AF470073

Jan Groth & Arne Adler

WHISKY & FOOD

For Hanna and Victor

MANY THANKS TO SIGMUND KAARSTAD AND DAVID MORTIMER-HAWKINS

PUBLISHED BY GRENADINE PUBLISHING 2011
GRENADINE PUBLISHING IS AN IMPRINT OF MASSOLIT PUBLISHING LTD.

WHISKY & FOOD

FIRST EDITION
ISBN 978-1-908233-04-2

ORIGINAL TITLE: WHISKY & MAT
TRANSLATION BY KATARINA SJÖWALL TRODDEN AND STEVALI PRODUCTION

ALL PHOTOGRAPHS BY ARNE ADLER

GRAPHIC DESIGN AND PRODUCTION: STEVALI PRODUCTION

PRINTED IN LATVIA BY LIVONIA PRINT 2011

GRENADINE PUBLISHING
6 ARTICHOKE MEWS
ARTICHOKE PLACE
LONDON SE5 8TS
UNITED KINGDOM
WWW.GRENADINE.SE

CONTENTS

WHISKY, FOOD AND PEOPLE

Many are those who have been inspired by the taste and aroma of whisky, especially single malts, since the mid-1990s. The unsurpassed flavour spectrum of whisky is becoming increasingly popular, and these days people meet up for tastings at virtually every street corner on a regular basis. They hold up their well-formed glasses to the light and contemplate the colour and nose, whether the flavours dominate at the front of the mouth or if they have a tendency to develop more slowly, causing unexpected sensations, further back. The skill and mastery of whisky enthusiasts are astonishing, and their desire to find out more about the secrets of single malts is impressive to say the least.

More and more people are also finding that even greater heights can be achieved when you add a companion food. I once met a man who told me about the evening he settled down with a bowl of popcorn and a glass of Glenburgie. All of a sudden something happened. The whisky flavours found their way to the browned butter and created a new, different and fascinating sensation. And once, during a tasting event, another man told me that his absolute favourite was whisky and *snus* tobacco, a combination that I can neither verify nor recommend since I have never tried it. This story prompted an elderly gentleman to stand up and explain that to him, the ultimate pleasure was to watch television in the company of a bag of sweets and a glass of Speyside. 'It's a question of letting the sweet dissolve in the whisky inside the mouth,' he cheerfully announced. These little stories, of course, tell us that everyone has their own likes and dislikes. No one is right, no one is wrong; although I would prefer not to pass comment on the *snus*/whisky combination.

Over the years, better qualified judges of taste than the ones mentioned above have spent hours and hours mulling over the way flavours work. In this book, I will be introducing some of the many tasty, inspiring flavour combinations in the world of food and whisky that have been created by a number of renowned Swedish chefs and food artists at my request. Their starting point was malt whisky, which was the intended drink to go with the meal. Numerous memorable works of art came as a result, created by chefs and food enthusiasts Daniel Karlsson, Eric Gadd, Anders Fridén, Andreas Nylén, Anders Levén and Roger Hjälm.

To all those chefs and whisky enthusiasts who have enriched my life by introducing flavours and providing inspiration, but who cannot be mentioned here due to the lack of space, I would like to say that you are not forgotten; get in touch, and we'll get together for a dram and a little something to eat.

Jan Groth

ANDERS FRIDÉN

ANDREAS NYLÉN

ANDERS LEVÉN

ERIC GADD

DANIEL KARLSSON

ROGER HJÄLM

JAN GROTH & ARNE ADLER

ONLY SCOTCH?

The purpose of this book is to explain the way Scottish single malts combine with different types of food. However, many excellent variations can be found outside Scotland. Ireland, for example, has long borne its whiskey traditions proudly, and the United States and Canada have a lot to offer, although they fall outside the scope of this book. One country that has come forward as a serious contender for Scotland's position in the Whisky Hall of Fame is Japan. Japanese whisky is multi-faceted, full-bodied and firmly based in the Scottish soil, which means that many of their bottled labels have similarities with whiskies we have learned to recognise as Scotch. Whisky from the Land of the Rising Sun goes extremely well with food, but I have chosen not to include any recipes or names, partly due to lack of space – they would fill an entire book – but also because many Japanese whiskies are still more difficult to get hold of than Scotch. Whisky is produced somewhat differently in the US. Bourbon is matured in new oak casks, which means that it is exposed to a different set of influences and therefore develops a different range of flavours. Each phase of the distillation process differs somewhat from the Scottish process, and the end result is different. Even though I have dedicated this chapter to explaining why I have chosen only to combine single malts produced in Scotland with food, I do not want to deprive you of a tasty, typically American combination, bourbon with Cajun food or BBQ – really delicious! I should add that I have decided to recommend only affordable whiskies that are easy to find.

WHISKY AND TASTE

There is no reason why whisky should not go well with food. Even though it may not be the first beverage that springs to mind as an accompaniment to venison or monkfish, the combination of food and whisky is not entirely alien to us. Every now and then, whisky turns up as an ingredient in cookery books or recipe collections. It is normally found in sauces or marinades, but occasionally it is used as a cheese flavouring or flambé spirit. Sorbets and other types of desserts are happy to make the acquaintance too, but let's be honest, in the last ten years or so whisky has not been universally accepted as a flavour enhancer, and even less as a table drink.

Without pretending to know much about the subject, I would like to claim that whisky has not been widely accepted as a table drink in the past either, except, of course, as an accompaniment to the traditional haggis. Even though I have met several Scottish farmers who pour scotch on their porridge oats even in this day and age, they seem to be more representative of the exception than the rule, and I am rather doubtful as to the authenticity of their early morning habits. The faintest of smiles leads me to suspect that it is partly done to give the Swedish tourist something to talk about back home. If you were to speculate on how whisky was consumed in pre-industrial Scotland, you would probably find that it was drunk in the same way as vodka or aquavit in Northern Europe. That is to say before, after and during a meal, regardless of whether it agreed with the food or not.

The idea of serving malt whisky with food requires certain additional facts, as it were. Your guests are not likely to get the point straight away, but beneath the alcohol and the prejudice, single malts harbour a vast variety of flavours. Once you have talked your friends into trying it, and after they have made the effort to do so, most of them will consider the experiment not only well worth the effort, but also delicious and inspiring.

When I drink whisky with food, I usually add a little chilled water. It releases all the individual flavours before they reach the palate and taste buds. Diluted malt whisky is smoother and easier to tolerate. When taken neat, it tends to fire on all cylinders at once, not allowing the more humble aromas generated by the herbs or spices to come forward. However, since most of these flavour combinations are relatively new experiences, I need to feel my way ahead with an open mind. However, some combinations require neat whisky, especially cheese and fatty fish.

AN INTRODUCTION TO A WORLD OF FLAVOURS

Single malts, although rich in flavours, are relatively straightforward. Imagine a motorway with few bends where all types of vehicles are permitted and where cars seldom drive off the road. In a blended whisky, on the other hand, the flavours of the ditch marry the entire spectrum of the forest, allowing you to distinguish an unlimited range of sensations. The individual notes are harder to make out, however, since they are affected by the presence of grain whisky. Single malts keep to the straight and narrow road, which is crowded and attractive in all its diversity. The number of discernible flavours within the aroma spectrum is almost unlimited, and the range of sensations becomes even more diverse in combination with food. However, an excellent single malt can also, believe it or not, be stripped to the bone and become flat and utterly pointless in the wrong company.

Flavours are formed more or less by accident during the manufacturing process. Taste molecules appear unexpectedly and often at random. I once had to explain to an obstinate participant at a whisky tasting event that the Scots do not add banana at any stage of the process, and that the banana marshmallow note is the result of a chemical reaction between the oak cask and the spirits.

It is relatively easy to distinguish the main ingredients in the whisky, that is to say the barley and malt notes. They are very common, and most of us can find them. The smoky notes are also easy to pick up. These flavours are created during the malting process when peat smoke contributes to one of the most distinct single malt styles. We are also able to easily discern various fruity flavours (although they are not always easy to name), while salt, pepper, leather, butter scotch, chocolate, nuts, furniture polish and a number of more or less specified notes are harder to find, and different people will react differently, at the same time as these flavours open up delightful possibilities. When and where during the process they form is currently being investigated. There is no doubt that most flavours are born during malting and fermenting. The shape and size of the copper stills determine which molecule chains will be refined, reformed, reproduced and deemed fit to pass through the condenser, and are thus important factors when it comes to the character of the distilled result. The condenser too, contributes a great deal to the taste and type of product. Experienced craftsmen contribute to giving the whisky its unique qualities, which are specific to each distillery. Moreover, the number of years the spirits have been stored in oak casks, which are normally imported from the United States (bourbon casks) or Europe (usually sherry casks), is a factor we have learned to appreciate. As you can see, there

is plenty of opportunity for flavours and aromas to develop. Would it not be great to be able to join a flavour on its ride on the rollercoaster, from ripe grain of barley to a molecule chain made up of a fascinating long aftertaste consisting of passion fruit followed by nutty, creamy vanilla and honey tones with a hint of orange, or even a fruit drop that takes us back to the days of our childhood.

All this tells us that finding a way of combining whisky with food is not an easy task, but the challenge allows us to imagine the results that may emerge in the end. Bottled single malts offer a whole range of flavours and aromas, but, as I mentioned earlier, they may completely lose all their distinguishing features in the wrong company. This is why experimenting is as important as it is fun. Use my suggestions as starting points, but make sure that you continue to develop your range of tastes. We are attracted by millions of flavours offered by new foods and spices every day. Be bold and discover how the good old single malt can get along with contemporary cuisine.

WHISKY DINNER

Although not an everyday occurrence, whisky dinners have become popular events in Scotland. The Scots have come to realise the value of their liquid heritage, and that it is possible to enjoy whisky in more ways than sipping it in a comfortable chair in front of the fire. Normally, these meals are created by whisky enthusiasts and innovative chefs. The more new flavours that enter the Scottish culinary scene, the better are the chances of matching full-bodied single malts with Indian, Japanese, Italian and other cuisines. Single malt is a worthy contender. These days, the choice of bottled malts on offer compares very well to other table drinks.

A whisky dinner tends to be a major undertaking. There is no getting away from it. But the result is tremendously exciting and the experience life enhancing for all the senses. You can of course pick one, even two, courses and serve them with whisky. This is in no way inferior, but it is not the same at all. A whisky dinner comprises at least one appetizer, one or two starters, one or two main courses and at least one flavour-rich dessert followed by coffee and more whisky. However, the point is not to fill the glasses to the brim while the main course goes stale on the table in front of you. Make sure to put plenty of water on the table. If you get thirsty you must drink water, not Lagavulin. Also make sure there is enough water for the whisky as well as for quenching your thirst. A whisky dinner is all about flavours and having a great time in good company.

In order to avoid misunderstandings and irritation, you will need to explain to your guests that they are invited to a whisky dinner. Try to serve the whisky in a different type of glass with each course as you would have done with wine. Serving the whisky that goes with the appetizer in a champagne flute is more festive than if it were served in a traditional whisky glass, and it will add to the overall experience. An attractive table setting and flawless preparation are musts for the success of your whisky dinner.

The food, which is of course one of the main attractions, must be carefully chosen to accompany the whiskies you will be serving. It is usually easier to find green vegetables, fruits and seasonings that match the flavours on which your meal is based. It is more difficult to start to prepare a course and then try to find a suitable single malt to go with it. It requires a well stocked bar cabinet. Instead, start by choosing a whisky you think is suitable, for example, a sweet Speyside. Then look for fish, seafood, fowl or meat to go with it. Build your meal around one ingredient and add green and root vegetables or other flavour enhancing foods. Finally, season the dish according to taste. This method is rather like the way a master blender creates a blended Scotch.

Some questions and answers:

SHOULD YOU AVOID FULL-BODIED MALTS AT THE BEGINNING OF DINNER?

Yes, normally you should, but it is not a rule. Each single malt performs unexpectedly and surprisingly in combination with food. Do not expect a full-bodied, oily whisky to always dominate and take over. Sometimes it simply falls into place without any fuss and adds to the overall experience.

CAN I INVITE PEOPLE TO A TRADITIONAL MEAL AND EXPECT TO FIND A SUITABLE WHISKY TO GO WITH IT?

Of course you can, if you have plenty of both time and whisky. One way of helping the meal along is to season the food with some of the whisky you are going to serve with the meal. It often, but not always, contributes to the overall harmony.

CAN YOU SERVE ANY BEVERAGE OTHER THAN WHISKY AT A WHISKY DINNER?

Yes! Water.

SHOULD NEW GLASSES BE SET OUT FOR EACH COURSE?

Yes, why not! Your guests may discover great flavour combinations that you have missed during the course of the meal. A whisky that was meant to go with the starter may find a suitable partner among the cheeses. All beverages tend to taste differently depending on what type of glass they are served in, which adds to the range of flavours and aromas.

HOW MUCH WHISKY SHOULD YOU POUR?

A seven-course whisky dinner ought to be accompanied by at the most two or three centilitres of whisky per course. Add water and quench your thirst with water. Serve a little more if there are fewer courses.

DO YOU NEED TO SERVE A DIFFERENT TYPE OF WHISKY WITH EACH COURSE?

No, you can serve the same type with more than one course.

DO YOU NEED TO WEAR A KILT DURING DINNER?

No, I do not think so.

Trust your own judgement and your taste buds; begin by serving straightforward flavours and keep adding flavours if you feel like it. Do not forget to keep tasting the food and drink during preparation and planning, it will make the whole procedure a lot more fun. Sometimes the planning of a whisky dinner is just as enjoyable as the meal itself!

The Swedish catering firm Taste It, with creative chef Roger Hjälm at the helm, accepted my request for a whisky dinner, and his team of cheerful, dedicated chefs enthusiastically took on the task. The number of culinary challenges and the number of working hours are always equal the number of laughs in their kitchen. When I first met them, they modestly suggested that they had no idea of how to combine single malts with the ingredients they were used to work with, but they accepted the challenge without hesitation. And, to be honest, there was little I could do to help.

'Above all,' says Roger Hjälm, 'it was hard to find suitable combinations, since we all had our own, preconceived ideas about what whisky tastes like, which meant that we thought that we knew what flavours were out of the question. As it turned out, we were far off the mark,' he explains. 'It was as if the whisky ceased to be whisky after a while and turned into familiar, well-defined flavours that changed and transformed, accepted or rejected the spices, or suddenly went overboard completely and started to dominate. We looked through our old recipes and tried to imagine how they would go with whisky, that is to say the labels we knew and appreciated. We often failed because we thought we knew what it would be like in advance. A trained chef can easily create simple flavour combinations using wine, but no preconceived ideas matched the flavour spectrum found in a single malt. Something that was surprising and extremely annoying,' says Roger, 'was that it was our trainee chef who discovered the best liked combination: one that we had rejected, even ridiculed, before we had even tried it.'

Most typical of Taste Its' initial problems was the fact that we humans are naturally lazy and tend to rely on what is familiar and recognisable. This is why these brilliant chefs did not choose Lagavulin; they knew it would probably kill anything that was served with it. The only one who tried it was the trainee, who had never tasted whisky before and who therefore did not know what to expect.

'It was bloody good,' says Roger. 'The whisky married the hickory, the maritime flavours and the sweetness of the apple. With hindsight, it is quite obvious.'

Recipes for a successful whisky dinner

REMEMBER TO SERVE THE WHISKY AT DIFFERENT TEMPERATURES AND IN DIFFERENT TYPES OF GLASS. EXPERIMENT AND BE BOLD ENOUGH TO OFFER A SURPRISE OR TWO.

HICKORY-SMOKED SALMON WITH APPLE SALSA

Instructions:

SALMON: Prepare the salmon by removing all bones and excess fat. Cut it into portion-sized pieces, 70 x 40 mm, and place them in a tin.

APPLE SALSA: Thereafter, chop apples and red onions into small, evenly-sized dices. Put them aside in a bowl. Pinch off dill from the stems and roll it up into a ball which you chop finely. Add to the apples and chilli sauce and mix.

Put a small dollop of apple salsa on each salmon piece and put them aside for a while. Place the hickory chips in a tin and preheat the oven to 250°C. Turn off the oven when the chips start producing smoke.

Put the salmon into the smoke in the oven. It is cooked when the inner temperature reaches 45°C.

Serve with a mixed herb salad.

WHISKY SUGGESTION: Lagavulin 16 with a little cool water

Serves 6–8

LAGAVULIN 16 YO WHISKY

1 KG SALMON
2 APPLES (PREFERABLY ROYAL GALA)
1 RED ONION
1 BUNCH OF DILL
2 TBSP SWEET CHILLI SAUCE
HICKORY CHIPS
SALT AND BLACK PEPPER

WHITE RADISH ROLLS WITH SOY JELLY SORBET AND GINGER

Instructions:

RADISH ROLLS: Peel the radish and slice it thinly. Peel the carrot and cut into sticks. Cut the pepper into sticks. Slice the salmon if needed and cut each slice in half. Place the thin radish slices on a tray and cover each with a slice of salmon. Roll up the salmon and do the same with the carrot, pepper and chives. Finish off with a small leaf of Lollo Biondo. Slice off the ends of the rolls. Finish by cutting up the rolls diagonally.

SOY JELLY: Combine soy sauce, vinegar and chilli sauce in a saucepan and bring to a boil. Leave gelatine leaves to soak in cold water for 5 minutes. Squeeze out the water and let the sheets dissolve in the hot soy sauce mixture. Pour everything into a tin covered in cling film, and put in the fridge until the jelly is set, approximately 3 hours. Lift out the jelly and cut it into cubes. Place salmon rolls and jelly cubes on a plate. Pipe some wasabi onto each cube.

GINGER SORBET: Peel the ginger and grate it finely. Let it boil with water and sugar for 10 minutes, allow to cool off and strain. Mix it with Sprite, lime juice and glucose. Let the gelatine soak in water for 5 minutes, squeeze out the water and let it dissolve without bringing it to a boil. Stir down the gelatine into the sorbet mixture. Let it cool off before putting it in the freezer.

WHISKY SUGGESTION: Chilled Dalwhinnie 15 YO in a white wine glass

DALWHINNIE 15 YO WHISKY

Serves 4

WHITE RADISH ROLL

½ WHITE RADISH
1 CARROT
1 YELLOW PEPPER
1 RED PEPPER
500 G SMOKED SALMON OR GRAVLAX
1 BUNCH CHIVES
4 LEAVES LOLLO BIONDO SALAD

SOY JELLY

100 ML KIKKOMAN SOY SAUCE
2 TBSP RICE VINEGAR
1 TBSP SWEET CHILLI SAUCE
4 GELATINE LEAVES
WASABI

GINGER SORBET

120 G FRESH GINGER
500 ML WATER
150 G CASTER SUGAR
300 ML SPRITE
2 LIMES
100 ML GLUCOSE
2 GELATINE LEAVES

SWEET-AND-SALTY DUCK BREASTS

Instructions:

DUCK BREASTS: Start by trimming the duck breasts of all skin and sinews. Score a criss-cross pattern into the fat. Put the breasts in a tin and add sugar and salt. Leave it in the fridge until the next day. Place the breasts in the pan with the fat side facing down and sear until browned. Add pepper. Roast in the oven at 100°C until it reaches a core temperature of 52°C. Let the meat cool down in tin foil for 5–10 minutes before serving.

RED WINE SAUCE: Chop onions, parsnip and garlic finely. Fry in oil. Sprinkle sugar on top and let it dissolve. Add red wine and balsamic vinegar and boil until half of the liquid remains. Add veal stock, salt and pepper to taste. Use a hand blender to make the sauce smooth. Add Caol Ila to taste. Thicken the sauce with cornflour if desired.

TERRINE: Cook the beetroots until soft, retaining their skins. Peel them and mash in a food processor. Add salt and pepper to taste. Put everything in a kitchen towel to drain excess liquid and refrigerate until cool. Boil potatoes until soft, retaining their skins. Peel and cut into smaller pieces. Fry the potatoes in plenty of butter until brown. Add salt and pepper to taste. Cover a baking tin with cling film. Stuff it densely with fried potatoes and refrigerate until the next day. Spread a thin layer of beetroot mash on top of the potatoes and refrigerate for another 2 hours. Using the cling film, lift out the terrine and cut it into portion-sized pieces. Immediately before serving, heat in oven for 15–20 minutes at 150°C.

WHISKY SUGGESTION: Caol Ila 12 YO with water in a red wine glass

CAOL ILA 12 YO WHISKY

Serves 4

PREPARE THE DAY BEFORE SERVING

DUCK BREASTS

5 BREASTS OF DUCK
200 ML SUGAR
50 ML SALT
BLACK PEPPER

RED WINE SAUCE WITH CAOL ILA

1 YELLOW ONION
1 PARSNIP
3 CLOVES OF GARLIC
2 TBSP OIL
100 ML CASTER SUGAR
200 ML RED WINE
4 TBSP BALSAMIC VINEGAR
3 TBSP VEAL STOCK
2 TBSP CAOL ILA
CORNFLOUR

BEETROOT AND POTATO TERRINE

500 G BEETROOTS
1 ½ KG POTATOES
400 G BUTTER
SALT AND BLACK PEPPER

PARMESAN SOUP

Instructions:

Bring milk and cream to a boil. Press the garlic, grate the parmesan and add to the pot. Use a hand blender to make the soup smooth. Add truffle oil, salt and pepper to taste. Bring the soup to a boil again and add Talisker to taste.

Leave the soup in the fridge until the next day. If needed, blend the soup one more time before serving. Serve with croutons, preferably of dark rye bread.

WHISKY SUGGESTION: Talisker 57 North with water in a dessert wine glass

Serves 4 as starter

300 ML DOUBLE CREAM
300 ML MILK
4 CLOVES OF GARLIC
200 ML GRATED PARMESAN CHEESE
2 TSP WHITE TRUFFLE OIL
SALT AND WHITE PEPPER
TALISKER TO TASTE
CROUTONS FOR SERVING

VANILLA BRÛLÉE

Instructions:

Preheat the oven to 150°C, or 125°C if using a hot-air oven, and place a pan of water in it at the same time.

Mix caster sugar, cream and milk in a pot. Slice up the vanilla pods and scrape out the seeds into the milk, thereafter add the pods themselves.

Bring the milk to a boil while stirring it. Put it aside to cool off before adding the eggs. Be careful not to whip it as this may cause bubbles to develop.

Strain and pour into smaller dishes, each containing about 100 ml.

Place the dishes in the water-bath in the oven, cover the pan with tin foil and bake for about 1 hour and 20 minutes.

Carefully take out the pan and allow the dishes to cool off in the water-bath. Put them in the fridge, preferably over night.

Sprinkle brown sugar on top of the brûlées and use a torch to melt it, alternatively, place the dishes high up in the oven on grill until the sugar is brown and crispy.

WHISKY SUGGESTION: Ice-cold Dalwhinnie 15 YO

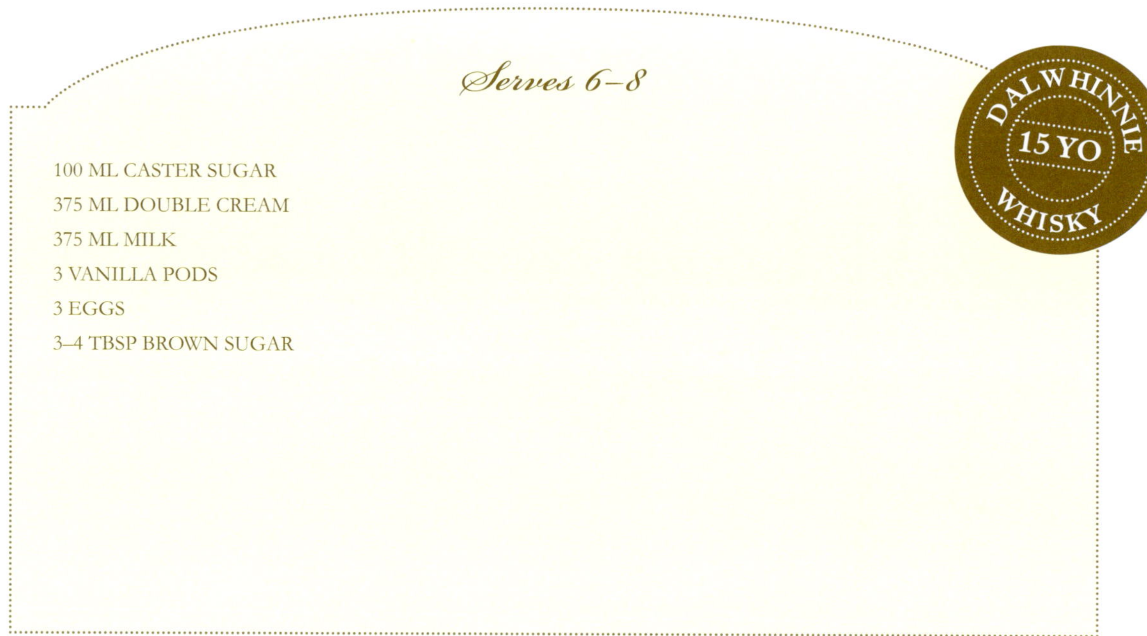

Serves 6–8

100 ML CASTER SUGAR
375 ML DOUBLE CREAM
375 ML MILK
3 VANILLA PODS
3 EGGS
3–4 TBSP BROWN SUGAR

Finish off with a selection of cheeses. See the chapter on whisky and cheese.

GOOD LUCK, AND DO NOT FORGET THAT THIS IS ALL ABOUT FLAVOURS AND ENJOYING THE COMPANY OF FRIENDS.

Saint Agur

SINGLE MALTS AND SNACKS

When it comes to combining whisky and food, one of my main strategies is that the contents of my drinks cabinet must be easily combined with whatever I happen to have in the fridge without interfering too much with my meal plans. I enjoy putting together simple, easily accomplished combinations. Olives or a piece of cheese that happen to go with a bottle of whisky I have sitting around at home, for example; and should I manage to rustle up some Parma ham or spicy sausage, it is even more exciting. You will inevitably find that certain combinations work better and are easier to get your head around than others. If you are planning a dinner party with friends, I recommend that you go for flavours that are not too demanding for sensitive palates. Trial and error is the best way forward.

I personally prefer simple combinations, and by simple I mean foods that do not require cooking or lengthy preparation. I often enjoy a fine single malt with some simple snack I have dug out of the fridge or larder. I should add, however, that this method has resulted in some pretty awful combinations, too. A piece of salmon always comes in handy, though. Cold-smoked salmon goes particularly well with most single malts, gravlax may work too. Imagine inviting a group of friends to the first barbeque of the season. The guests start to arrive, they are looking forward to the evening, they are all a little curious, and you serve them a starter consisting of cold-smoked salmon on white bread or cut in cubes held together by a skewer. As an accompaniment, you offer them Talisker and a little water served in a champagne flute. Your friends will no doubt raise an eyebrow or two. The conversation flows, it will be an evening to remember. If you are feeling bold, oysters with the traditional Tabasco or lemon replaced by whisky will definitely get people talking.

As the evening progresses, why not serve pieces of preserved ginger with a glass of Oban. Unforgettable!

Round the evening off with a well-filled cheese platter. Discreetly produce a bottle of Laphroaig and ask your guests to sample the sensational combination. But do not expect whisky to be everyone's beverage of choice with St Augur or Stilton, although those who are brave enough to try it will not be disappointed.

As you will have discovered by now, this chapter is about serving simple snacks with small glasses of whisky. Just imagine the possibilities: a selection of single malts in your drinks cabinet and a variation of flavours in the fridge and larder. Kay Fleming, production manager at Glenkinchie, once told me a story about how a piece of plain chocolate once did the thing for a game of curling and got her some friends for life on the bowling green.

'I used to work at Brora in the north of Scotland,' she says, 'and we used to play curling. In the winter, when it was really cold, we would bring a "packed lunch" consisting

of a thermos flask filled with our favourite malt whisky. Once someone offered me a Malteser, which I enjoyed. Then, with the sweet still in my mouth, I took a sweep from my flask, which happened to contain Caol Ila. The result was overwhelming. I offered some to everyone in my team, and we won hands over. If it was due to the chocolate or to the whisky I don't know, but I had definitely discovered my favourite combination. Later, when I was working at Glenkinchie where curling sheets where usually green and ice-free, I had almost forgotten about my favourite combination, but there was a garden with a bowling green at the distillery, and when the staff met a neighbouring firm I remembered my experience of Caol Ila and Maltesers. It worked in East Lothian too. We won the game, and I acquired several new friends. I call it The Delish Dish,' says Kay with a smile. Another happy coincidence!

The message is simple: do not be afraid of experimenting, and use your imagination. The following recipes and suggestions have been tried and enjoyed by whisky-loving friends in Sweden and Scotland. The concept is a new one, however, and many paths are still unexplored. Be confident and try your own combinations. Starters and snacks are always appreciated, and do serve the whisky in different types of glass. Best of luck and enjoy.

Appetizers and fingerfood

PICTURE THE FIRST BBQ NIGHT OF THE YEAR, ON THE PORCH OR IN THE GARDEN. THE GUESTS START TO ARRIVE AND YOU SERVE THEM COLD SMOKED SALMON AND A CHAMPAGNE GLASS. IMAGINE THEIR SURPRISE WHEN THEY DISCOVER THAT THE GLASS CONTAINS NOT WINE BUT TALISKER SINGLE MALT WHISKY!

WHISKY-CURED GRAVLAX

Instructions:

Mix salt, sugar and pepper in a bowl. Sprinkle half of the mixture in the bottom of a tin. Put the salmon on top and use a pastry brush to cover it with Talisker. Thereafter, sprinkle the rest of the mixture on top, as well as the dill. Cover the tin with cling film and refrigerate for 2–3 days. Turn over the salmon a few times during this time. Serve the salmon on thin crisp bread.

WHISKY SUGGESTION: Talisker 10 YO

Serves 6

TALISKER 10 YO WHISKY

1 KG SALMON
2 TSP COARSELY GROUND WHITE PEPPER
50 ML SALT
50 ML SUGAR
DILL
3 TBSP TALISKER 10 YO

SALMON SPREAD

Instructions:

Peel the apple and dice it finely. Dice the salmon. Mix salmon, apple and mayonnaise in a bowl and add dill, pepper and a pinch of salt. Form small balls and put them on slices of dark rye bread.

Squeeze plenty of lemon juice and sprinkle some sea salt on top immediately before serving. This is an unusual and easy-to-make appetizer that surprises on a warm summer day.

WHISKY SUGGESTION: Talisker 18 YO

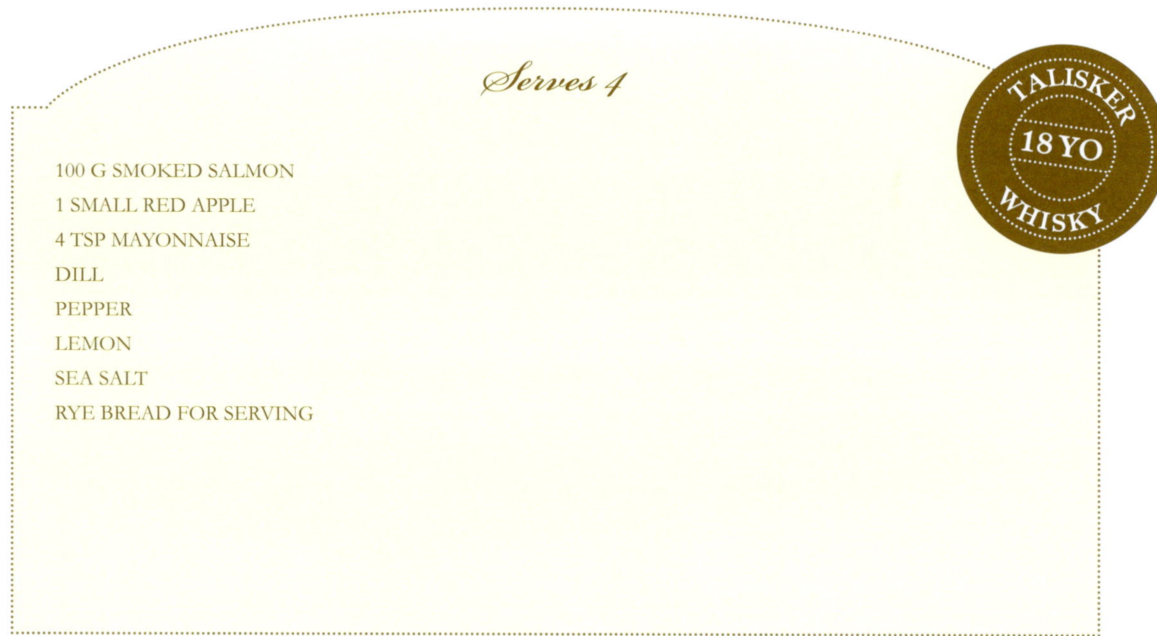

Serves 4

100 G SMOKED SALMON
1 SMALL RED APPLE
4 TSP MAYONNAISE
DILL
PEPPER
LEMON
SEA SALT
RYE BREAD FOR SERVING

THE WHISKY AND THE SEA

Instructions:

Leave the seaweed to soak in water. When they start turning green and have swelled up a bit, squeeze them dry. Fry the seaweed with the finely chopped shallots in olive oil. Add a splash of Talisker. Let everything cool off. Cut the rollmops into portion-sized pieces.

Place the seaweed on a plate, add the fish and finish off by drizzling crème fraiche on top. A Scandinavian-style summer snack that is bound to raise a few eyebrows.

WHISKY SUGGESTION: Talisker 10 YO

Serves 4

160 G DRIED SEAWEED
320 G ROLLMOPS
200 ML CRÈME FRAICHE
2 SHALLOTS
OLIVE OIL
TALISKER 10 YO

SCALLOP CARPACCIO WITH APPLE AND OBAN JELLY

Instructions:

Put the scallops in the freezer for a little while – this makes it easier to slice them thinly.

JELLY: Start by pouring apple cordial into a pot. Heat it up without allowing it to boil. Add Oban to taste. You should strive for a rich and pleasant balance between whisky and apple flavours. Add gelatine leaves (follow the instructions on the box for proper dosage).

When the sheets have dissolved, take the saucepan off the heat and pour contents into attractive whisky or schnapps glasses until set.

SCALLOPS: Slice scallops thinly and put them on a plate. Serve with jelly and garnish with chives. Enjoy!

WHISKY SUGGESTION: Oban 14 YO

Serves 2

100 ML APPLE CORDIAL
GELATINE LEAVES
4 FRESH SCALLOPS
OBAN 14 YO
CHIVES

MINI BEEF PASTRAMI SANDWICHES WITH WHISKY-PICKLED CHANTERELLES

Instructions:

MUSHROOMS: Bring whisky, vinegar essence, sugar and water to a boil. Put mushrooms in a bowl and pour the hot syrup on top. Leave until cool.

DRESSING: Mix egg yolks with vinegar and add oil drop by drop until thick. If too thick, dilute with water. Add salt and pepper to taste.

SANDWICHES: Toss the rocket in some hazelnut dressing. Put the pastrami slices on a plate and distribute the salad on top of the meat. Roll into cones. Put the rolls on the bread slices and sprinkle the whisky-pickled mushrooms on top. These mini sandwiches make perfect hors-d'oeuvres. You can replace fresh chanterelles with deep-frozen, but make sure they are properly drained first.

WHISKY SUGGESTION: Knockando 12 YO

12 mini sandwiches

SANDWICHES

12 SLICES BEEF PASTRAMI
12 SLICES DARK RYE BREAD
100 G ROCKET

WHISKY-PICKLED CHANTERELLES

1 ½ TBSP KNOCKANDO 12 YO
50 ML WHITE VINEGAR ESSENCE
100 ML CASTER SUGAR
200 ML SMALL CHANTERELLES (APPROX. 100 G)

HAZELNUT DRESSING

2 EGG YOLKS
1 TBSP CHAMPAGNE VINEGAR OR APPLE CIDER VINEGAR
200 ML HAZELNUT OIL
50 ML WATER
½ TSP SALT
1 PINCH FRESHLY GROUND BLACK PEPPER

PAN-FRIED SCALLOPS WITH MORNAY SAUCE AND CRANBERRY SYRUP

Instructions:

SCALLOPS: Fry the scallops in lightly browned butter in a pan. Add salt and pepper. Take off the heat and leave to cool.

CRANBERRY SYRUP: Let cranberries, sugar and water boil on medium heat for about 10 minutes. Pour some of the liquid onto a cold plate to test its thickness when cool. It should be similar to syrup in thickness. Strain through a sieve. Leave to cool in the refrigerator.

MORNAY SAUCE: Bring whisky to a boil, add milk and bring to a boil again. Use the cornflour to thicken the sauce. Add parmesan, salt and freshly ground white pepper to taste.

Heat up the scallops in the oven at 220°C for about 3 minutes before serving. Pour some sauce on a plate and use a spoon to make a trail in the middle. Pour some cranberry syrup in the trail and garnish with fresh cranberries and salad. A very stylish dish that appeals to the eye as well as the palate.

WHISKY SUGGESTION: Oban 14 YO

Serves 4

OBAN 14 YO WHISKY

SCALLOPS
8 SCALLOPS WITHOUT THEIR MUSCLES
BUTTER FOR FRYING

CRANBERRY SYRUP
100 ML CRANBERRIES
75 ML CASTER SUGAR
50 ML WATER

MORNAY SAUCE
100 ML OBAN WHISKY
300 ML MILK
CORNFLOUR AS THICKENING AGENT
100 ML GRATED PARMESAN CHEESE
SALT AND FRESHLY GROUND WHITE PEPPER
MÂCHE SALAD FOR GARNISH

GRILLED OYSTERS WITH CHILLI SALSA

Instructions:

Open the oysters.

Core the tomato and dice it finely. Chop garlic finely.

Mix tomato, garlic and onion and add honey, Liquid Smoke, salt and pepper. Distribute the salsa on the oysters.

Grill the oysters for approximately 1 minute.

Serve the oysters directly from the grill with a glass of Lagavulin.

This recipe is a revelation for any lover of smoky whisky and refined food.

WHISKY SUGGESTION: Lagavulin 16 YO

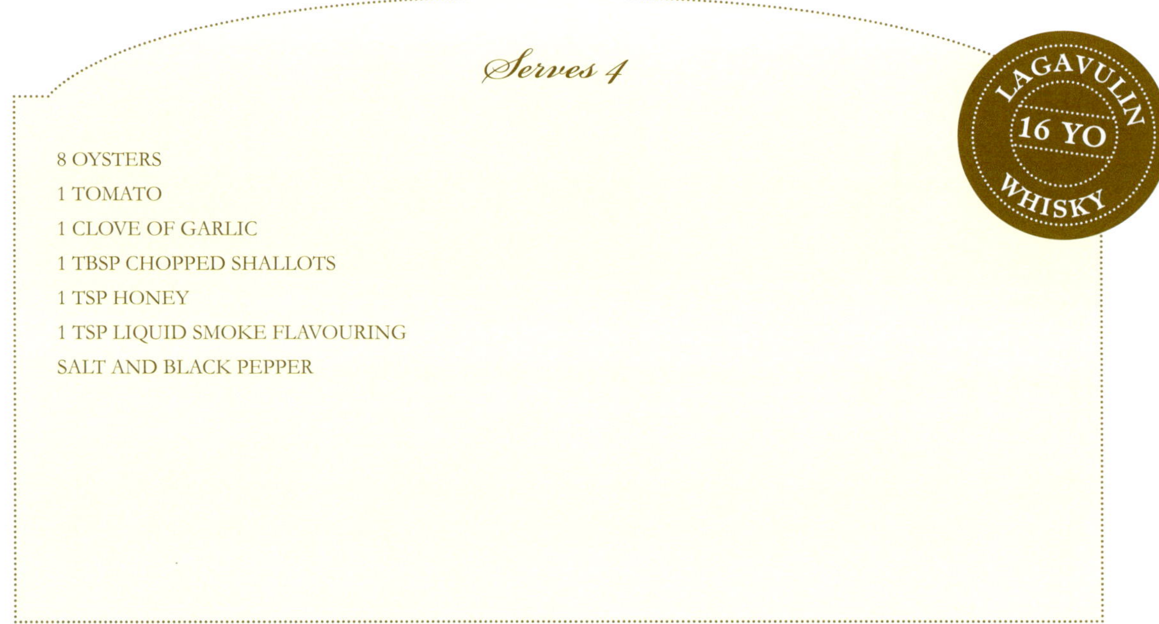

Serves 4

8 OYSTERS
1 TOMATO
1 CLOVE OF GARLIC
1 TBSP CHOPPED SHALLOTS
1 TSP HONEY
1 TSP LIQUID SMOKE FLAVOURING
SALT AND BLACK PEPPER

OYSTERS WITH ARDBEG FOAM

Instructions:

Mix whisky, water and lecithin (a natural fat based on soy, which can be bought in well-stocked shops) in a bowl.

Blend until you get a fluffy foam.

Serve the oysters with the foam on top. World class cuisine!

WHISKY SUGGESTION: Ardbeg 10 YO

Serves 4

8 OYSTERS
20 ML ARDBEG 10 YO
20 ML WATER
2 TSP LECITHIN

DUCK LIVER WITH FIG MARMALADE AND PICKLES

Prepare the day before serving

Instructions:

Start by chopping the duck liver coarsely. Thereafter, bring cream and whisky to a boil and add the chopped duck liver. Blend and add salt and pepper to taste. Strain the mixture and put it in a dish covered in cling film over night.

SERVING INSTRUCTIONS: Slice up the duck liver pâté and put it on plates. Serve with fig marmalade and pickles.

WHISKY SUGGESTION: Cragganmore 12 YO

Serves 4

160 G DUCK LIVER
50 ML DOUBLE CREAM
1 TBSP CRAGGANMORE
SALT AND BLACK PEPPER
PICKLES
FIG MARMALADE

CANAPÉ WITH SMOKED SHRIMPS

Instructions:

Peel and devein the shrimps. Chop red onion, spring onion and apple finely. Mix shrimps, red onion, spring onion and apple with the mayonnaise.

Cut the bread into thin circles and pan-fry it in butter.

Add a dollop of the shrimp spread on the fried bread and some roe on top.

Smoked shrimps can sometimes be bought in a delicatessen or fish market, but if they are hard to find you can smoke them yourself in the oven or a fish smoker.

WHISKY SUGGESTION: Glen Elgin

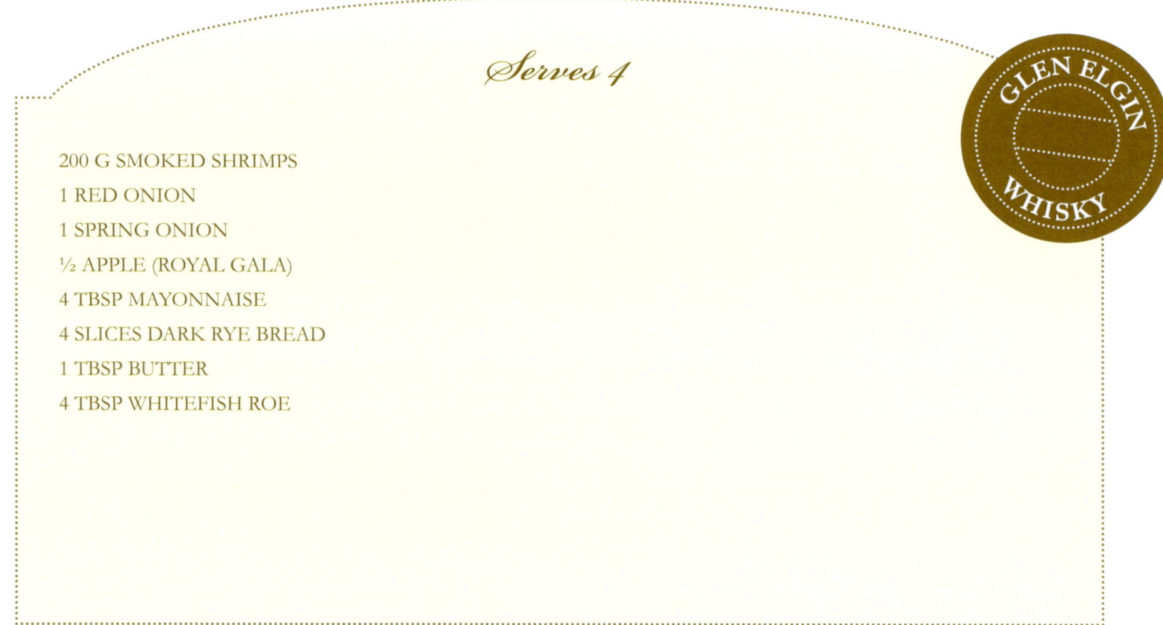

Serves 4

200 G SMOKED SHRIMPS
1 RED ONION
1 SPRING ONION
½ APPLE (ROYAL GALA)
4 TBSP MAYONNAISE
4 SLICES DARK RYE BREAD
1 TBSP BUTTER
4 TBSP WHITEFISH ROE

ROLLMOPS WITH FENNEL DRESSING, ROASTED PANCETTA AND GRILLED POTATOES

Instructions:

FENNEL DRESSING: Mix egg yolks with whisky, lemon juice and fennel seeds. Add the oil in a thin drizzle, whip until smooth. Add salt and pepper to taste.

ROLLMOPS: Cut the fillets diagonally into 12 pieces. Cut the boiled potatoes in 12 thick slices and grill them in a grill pan. Dry-fry the pancetta or bacon. Put one chard leaf on each potato slice, drizzle over the dressing and add a fish piece on top. Top with the pancetta.

This dish is best served room-tempered as an appetizer or a snack.

WHISKY SUGGESTION: Glenfiddich 12 YO

Serves 12 as starter

FENNEL DRESSING
- 2 EGG YOLKS
- 2 TBSP GLENFIDDICH 12 YO
- 1 TBSP LEMON JUICE
- 1 TBSP ROASTED FENNEL SEEDS
- 150 ML RAPESEED OIL
- 50 ML SESAME OIL
- ½ TSP SALT
- 1 PINCH FRESHLY GROUND WHITE PEPPER
- SWISS CHARD

ROLLMOPS
- 4 ROLLMOP FILLETS
- 6 LARGE BOILED POTATOES
- 50 G DICED PANCETTA OR BACON

GOATS' CHEESE ON FRUITY SALAD

Instructions:

Preheat the oven to 200°C. Cut the goats' cheese in slices, 5 mm thick, and leave them out in room temperature. Peel the mango and slice it very thinly. Peel the orange and section it, removing the membrane. Mix the mango slices and orange sections with the sugar and let them absorb the sugar for 30 minutes.

Cut the tortilla into squares. Put them on an oven tray covered in oven paper and drizzle olive oil on top. Sprinkle sea salt on top and bake in the oven for about 5 minutes until bread is crispy. Leave to cool.

Distribute rinsed salad on plates. Place the fruit on top, proceed with the bread and finish off with the goats' cheese. Garnish with dill. Serve immediately before the bread starts to soften.

WHISKY SUGGESTION: Glenmorangie Original

Serves 4

GLENMORANGIE ORIGINAL WHISKY

400 G GOATS' CHEESE
½ MANGO
1 ORANGE
2 TBSP BROWN SUGAR
1 WHEAT TORTILLA
OLIVE OIL
SEA SALT
10–12 MIXED SALAD LEAVES
FRESH DILL TO GARNISH

FUNNEL CHANTERELLE SOUP WITH RAINBOW TROUT TIMBALE AND APPLE JELLY

Instructions:

SOUP: Chop onion, garlic and parsnip finely. Fry in the oil with the mushrooms. Add white wine and let the liquid reduce to half. Add milk, cream and stock. Use a hand blender to make the soup smooth. Add salt, pepper and truffle oil to taste.

APPLE JELLY: Bring apple juice to a boil and add truffle oil. Let the gelatine soak. Squeeze it until dry and add it to the juice. Pour into small dishes and add the wood-sorrel. Put it somewhere cool. Before serving, warm the dish in water to loosen the jelly.

TIMBALE: Mix oil, egg yolk, mustard and honey to a mayonnaise, add salt and pepper to taste. Remove all the fish from the bones and put in a bowl. Dice the apple and ham in 3 mm sized cubes and add this to the fish. Chop the onion and wood-sorrel finely and combine with the fish and mayonnaise. Mix and add salt and pepper to taste. Stuff densely into dishes and refrigerate. Before serving, add some caviar on top of the timbale.

WHISKYTIPS: Dalhwinnie 15 YO

Serves 4

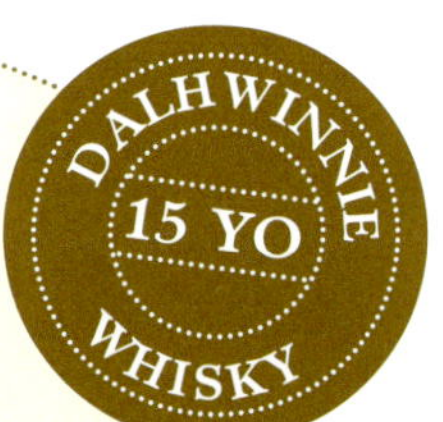

SOUP

1 YELLOW ONION
2 CLOVES OF GARLIC
½ PARSNIP
50 ML DRIED FUNNEL CHANTERELLES
1 TBSP RAPESEED OIL
100 ML WHITE WINE (PINOT GRIS ALSACE)
300 ML MILK
200 ML DOUBLE CREAM
3 TBSP CHICKEN STOCK
1 TSP TRUFFLE OIL
SALT AND WHITE PEPPER

APPLE JELLY

6 TBSP APPLE JUICE
1 TSP TRUFFLE OIL
1 GELATINE LEAF
3 WOOD-SORREL LEAVES

TIMBALE

100 ML OIL
1 EGG YOLK
1 TSP DIJON MUSTARD
1 TSP HONEY
SALT AND WHITE PEPPER
300 G SMOKED RAINBOW TROUT
1 APPLE
70 G SMOKED HAM
½ RED ONION
1 TSP WOOD-SORREL LEAVES, CHOPPED
SALT AND WHITE PEPPER
2 TBSP RAINBOW CAVIAR

INDEPENDENT BOTTLERS

Independent bottlers buy up whiskies that whisky producers for some inexplicable reason have decided not to bottle as single malts. Or, they acquire batches of new-make spirit from the distillery and choose their own casks and storage site. We owe a lot to these firms. Without them, the choice would have been a lot more limited. They have worked tirelessly to promote malt whisky throughout the world. Names like Cadenheads, Gordon & MacPhail, Adelphi, Duncan Taylor, Clydesdale and many more are music to the ears of a whisky lover. Small editions of sometimes idiosyncratic, but more often than not interesting experiences broaden the spectrum of flavours and aromas. Uniqueness is more important than continuity; each bottle must be one of a kind. Customers have to trust the reputation of the bottler rather than the often familiar name of the distillery. So, even though we may recognise the name of the distillery that produced the spirits, it does not mean that the content of a bottle from an independent bottler will be familiar – the number of editions is extensive and the bottlers' enthusiasm never fails to impress me. There are those who claim that without them, many single malt distilleries would have disappeared unnoticed.

Now that I have sung their praise, what do I have to say about the food/whisky combination? There is no room for a detailed account of these well-rounded flavours in a book of this kind. A bottle of twenty-two-year-old Caperdonich from a single barrel, bottled by one of the above-mentioned firms may turn out to be superb with a piece of fruit cake or a spiced cake and cheese. The problem is, however, that you are not likely to come across it more than once in a lifetime, if at all. The next bottle of Caperdonich you manage to find will offer an entirely different set of flavours, which means it will go better with something else. Finding a suitable recipe for a limited edition is not an easy task. Frequently, only one barrel is bottled, which means that the end product is tantalisingly unique, but since no two bottles are alike, it is hard to recommend it with any specific food in mind.

Nevertheless, I encourage anyone who owns a unique bottle of whisky to try and match it with various flavours and to use their imagination.

NEW DISTILLERIES

A steady stream of new flavours is created by distillers who like to contribute to the world of single malts. Their achievements are admirable and I applaud the samples I have managed to acquire, for example from Kilchoman on Islay, Arran (somewhat older), Daftmill or, for that matter from Glengyle of Campeltown and Mackmyra at Sandviken in Sweden. All are refreshing, well-stewed drops of malt that want nothing more than to continue to be cradled inside their oak barrels for some time yet. Naturally, new distillates from other countries are bringing some hope for the future too, but unfortunately they are all extremely hard to match with food, since the whiskies will change and flavours will combine in various ways over the next few years. New single malts can contribute to exciting food combinations, however, and are a constant topic of conversation. I once had the honour of listening and talking to the head of the Glengoyne visitors centre. She explained to me that one of her favourites was to lace her Christmas cake with very young malt whisky. She even recommended new-make, i.e. the distillate that has not yet earned the epithet 'whisky'.

A new distillery has been established on the island of Ven between Sweden and Denmark, which may, in future, become a talking point in Sweden. Welsh Penderyn and Indian Amrut have already won a few battles in the field. There are German, French and Finnish distilleries that produce good and, I have to admit, not so good, single malts.

I am constantly reading about new, exciting distillery projects in newsletters and books, but, again, I will not be mentioning any flavour combinations for them because they are not yet fully matured, and it would be unproductive to put a label on them at this early stage. I suggest you wait and see. The world is full of promising new ideas.

Since there are no geographical boundaries to whisky-making, we must not limit their development and appeal in the future. Do look back in time, but do not forget that the future will bring many exciting single malt and food combinations.

Main courses

MOST PEOPLE WILL PROBABLY ENJOY OTHER DRINKS WITH THE MAIN COURSES – BUT FOR THE BRAVE, MALT WHISKY IN COMBINATION WITH THESE RECIPES OFFERS A FASCINATING COMBINATION OF FLAVOURS.

WHISKY-STEAMED MUSSELS

Instructions:

Rinse the mussels to remove dirt and grime. Discard any mussels which are broken or do not close when tapped.

Dilute the whisky with water until you have approximately 200 ml liquid. Heat up the oil in a deep saucepan or casserole. Finely chop the onion and fry it in oil until soft. Fry the bacon gently with the onions, making sure it does not burn. Add the mussels and the diluted whisky. Place a lid on the saucepan and simmer for approximately 5 minutes until the mussels have opened.

Bring the saucepan to the table, open the lid, sprinkle chopped parsley on top and let the guests enjoy the smell. Serve immediately with rustic bread.

WHISKY SUGGESTION: Islay whisky

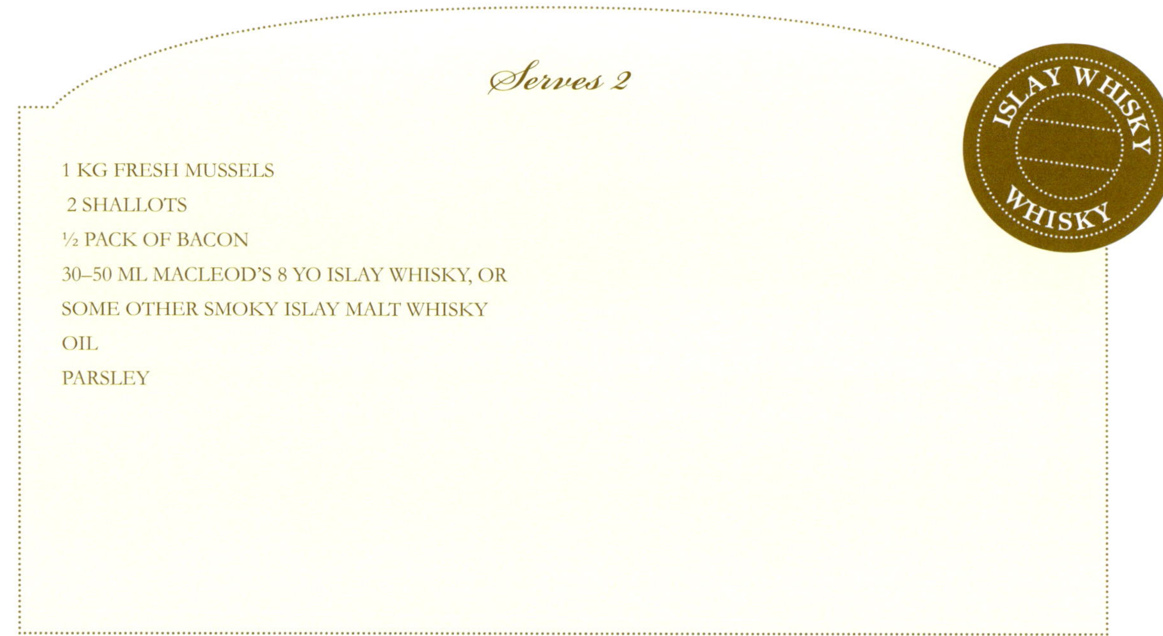

Serves 2

1 KG FRESH MUSSELS
2 SHALLOTS
½ PACK OF BACON
30–50 ML MACLEOD'S 8 YO ISLAY WHISKY, OR SOME OTHER SMOKY ISLAY MALT WHISKY
OIL
PARSLEY

CREAMY MUSSEL SOUP

Instructions:

Scrape out the mussels. Chop the shallots and fry them with thyme in olive oil. Add mussels and wine. Put a lid on and let it simmer for a few minutes until mussels have opened up. Add fish or crayfish stock and bring to a boil. The saltiness should be quite intense before adding the white chocolate. Try to find a nice balance between saltiness and sweetness. Add cream and blend.

Serve the mussel soup with a piece of whisky-cured gravlax and dark rye bread.

You will find the recipe for whisky-cured gravlax on page 38.

WHISKY SUGGESTION: Talisker 10 YO

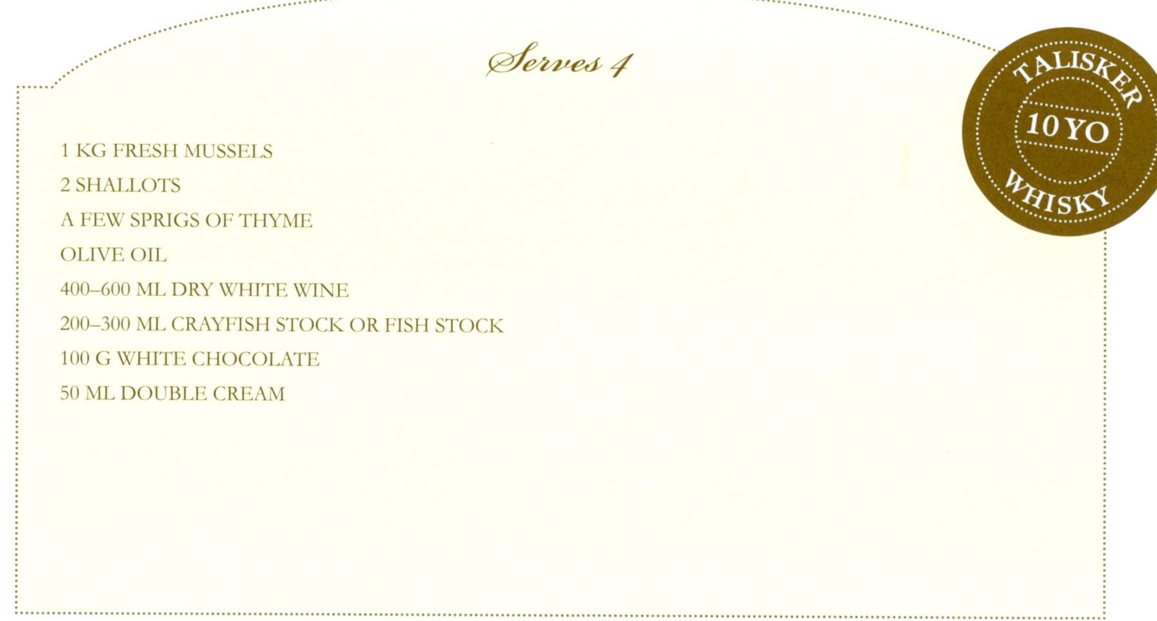

Serves 4

1 KG FRESH MUSSELS
2 SHALLOTS
A FEW SPRIGS OF THYME
OLIVE OIL
400–600 ML DRY WHITE WINE
200–300 ML CRAYFISH STOCK OR FISH STOCK
100 G WHITE CHOCOLATE
50 ML DOUBLE CREAM

WHISKY HALIBUT

Instructions:

HALIBUT: Marinate the halibut in soy sauce and Talisker for 1–2 days. Cut it into portion-sized pieces and fry them quickly in a pan before baking them in the oven until fully cooked. Dice chorizo sausage, red onion, fennel and mange-touts finely and let it sizzle in olive oil.

POTATO PUREE: Boil the potatoes until soft and pass them through a ricer. Heat up milk and butter. Mix and add parmesan, salt and pepper to taste.

RED WINE SAUCE: Chop onion, parsnip and garlic finely. Fry in oil. Add sugar and let it dissolve. Add red wine and balsamic vinegar and boil until half of the liquid remains. Add veal stock, salt and pepper to taste. Use a hand blender to make the sauce smooth. If needed, use cornflour to thicken the sauce. Add the orange juice and boil to desired thickness. Best served on beautiful china and accompanied by whisky in a red wine glass.

WHISKY SUGGESTION: Talisker Distillers' Edition

Serves 6

TALISKER DISTILLERS EDITION WHISKY

HALIBUT

1 KG HALIBUT
1 PART SOY SAUCE
4 PARTS TALISKER 10 YO
1 CHORIZO SAUSAGE
1 RED ONION
½ FENNEL
100 G MANGE-TOUTS

POTATO PUREE

1 KG POTATOES
350 ML MILK
125 G BUTTER
PARMESAN CHEESE
SALT AND PEPPER

ORANGE SAUCE

1 PART RED WINE SAUCE
2 PARTS FRESHLY SQUEEZED ORANGE JUICE

RED WINE SAUCE

1 YELLOW ONION
1 PARSNIP
3 CLOVES OF GARLIC
2 TBSP OIL
100 ML SUGAR
200 ML RED WINE
4 TBSP BALSAMIC VINEGAR
3 TBSP VEAL STOCK
CORNFLOUR AS THICKENING AGENT

10

LAMB FILLET "ON THE FIELD"

Instructions:

LAMB: Marinate the lamb fillets for 2 days in a marinade consisting of 1 part soy sauce and 4 parts Talisker 10 YO, thyme and garlic.

Let the meat sear in a frying pan on all sides and roast it in the oven until cooked to your preference.

POMMES ANNA: Slice the potatoes and onion thinly and fry them quickly with finely grated garlic. Cover an oven dish with cling film. Put potatoes and onions in layers with the cheese in the dish and add cream. Bake at 120°C for 1–1 ½ hours, or until set. Cover the potato cake with cling film and place something heavy on top to press it down, and let it cool off. Cut the potato cake in slices and fry.

Let the sauce boil until it reaches desired thickness. This dish can easily be made in smaller portions and be served as part of a buffet table.

WHISKY SUGGESTION: Talisker 10 YO

Serves 6

TALISKER 10 YO WHISKY

LAMB
1 KG LAMB FILLET
1 PART SOY SAUCE
4 PARTS TALISKER 10 YO
1 SPRIG OF THYME
GARLIC TO TASTE

POMMES ANNA
1 KG FLOURY POTATOES
1 YELLOW ONION
150 G MATURE HARD CHEESE
100–200 ML SINGLE CREAM
1 CLOVE OF GARLIC
BUTTER FOR FRYING

WHISKY SAUCE
2 PARTS TALISKER 10 YO
1 PART RED WINE SAUCE (RECIPE ON PAGE 74)

ONG 06°21'.5W

DUCK BREASTS WITH CHILLI AND CHOCOLATE SAUCE

Instructions:

PUMPKIN TORTILLA: Split the pumpkin in half. Scrape out the seeds and score a checked pattern into the flesh without cutting through the skin. Place the pumpkin in an oven dish and drizzle oil on top. Roast in the middle of the oven at 200°C for about 30 minutes. Let it cool off and scrape off the flesh. Mash with a hand blender. Add salt. Cut the courgette in long slices and fry in a pan until slightly soft. Heat the tortillas in a frying pan with some oil until light brown. Place a tortilla in a pie dish. Spread half of the pumpkin mash on top. Add another tortilla, courgette slices and sliced mozzarella cheese. Add salt and pepper. Add the rest of the pumpkin mash. Cover with a tortilla and flatten slightly. Bake in the lower part of the oven at 200°C for about 30 minutes.

SAUCE: Blanch and deseed the chilli, then mash it with a hand blender. Fry the onion in oil with the nuts. Add the chilli and fry it quickly. Add lager, tomatoes and stock. Bring to a boil. Then add the chocolate and honey. Let it simmer without lid for approximately 40 minutes. Give it a stir now and then. Dilute with stock or water if it looks too thick. Mash everything through a sieve and add salt, honey and whisky to taste.

DUCK BREASTS: Use a knife to score a criss-cross pattern into the fat of the duck breasts. Rub them with salt and place them in a hot frying pan with butter and oil. Fry quickly until browned and place them, fat side facing up, in a dish. Stick a meat thermometer into one of the breasts. Place the dish in the oven at 200°C and roast until the inner temperature reaches 62°C, which should take about 15 minutes. Take them out of the dish and let them rest for 5 minutes before cutting the meat. Serve with sauce, tortilla and broccoli.

WHISKY SUGGESTION: Talisker 10 YO

Serves 4

PUMPKIN TORTILLA
1 KG PUMPKIN FLESH
½ TBSP OLIVE OIL
SEA SALT
1 COURGETTE, ABOUT 400 G
3 LARGE, SOFT CORN TORTILLAS
2 BUFFALO MOZZARELLA CHEESES
SALT AND BLACK PEPPER

SAUCE
2 CHIPOTLE, 2 ANCHO AND 2 PASILLA CHILLI PEPPERS (OR ANCHO ONLY)
1 SHALLOT, FINELY CHOPPED
2 CLOVES OF GARLIC, FINELY CHOPPED
1 TBSP OIL
100 ML CHOPPED PEANUTS
1 BOTTLE (330 ML) LAGER
1 TIN OF CHOPPED TOMATOES
200 ML BEEF STOCK
100 G DARK CHOCOLATE, 70%
3 TBSP RUNNY HONEY
WHISKY

DUCK BREASTS
2 CLEAN DUCK BREASTS, WITH RIND
½–1 TSP SEA SALT
½ TBSP BUTTER + ½ TBSP OIL

COD FILLET WITH PINE NUTS

Instructions:

Cut the cod into serving pieces. Mix all ingredients for the marinade and bring them to a boil. Place the fish pieces in the warm marinade and turn them over, but no longer than a minute as the fish may overcook and fall apart. It should be almost like sushi fish. Lift up the pieces one by one and put them on a plate.

Let the marinade cool off, to be used later for serving. Split the cucumber lengthwise. Use a sharp knife or a cheese slicer to cut out four slices lengthwise and put one on each plate.

Distribute the cod on the cucumber slices and dribble a teaspoon of the marinade on each piece. Garnish with chilli, pine nuts and a dollop of yoghurt.

WHISKY SUGGESTION: Clynelish 14 YO

Serves 4

COD

400 G COD FILLETS, SKINLESS AND BONELESS

MARINADE

2 TBSP LIGHT CHINESE SOY SAUCE
2 TBSP RUNNY HONEY
1 TBSP HOISIN SAUCE
1 TSP RED CHILLI OIL (CHILLI-INFUSED OLIVE OIL)
1 TBSP SESAME OIL

FOR SERVING

1 CUCUMBER
1 RED CHILLI, FINELY CHOPPED
50 G PINE NUTS, ROASTED
200 ML GREEK OR TURKISH YOGHURT, DRAINED

GRILLED T-BONE STEAK WITH HOT 'N' SMOKY SWEET CORN BUTTER

Instructions:

BUTTER: Preheat the oven to 175°C. Roast the sweet corn it they adapts a deep yellow and most of the liquid has evaporated. Stir from time to time to ensure that they do not stick. Using a hand blender, mix the sweet corn, chilli and a pinch of sea salt, and add whisky until nice and smoky. Whip the butter until light and fluffy, add the mixture and stir gently.

STEAK: Grill the T-bone steaks on a coal grill or grill pan.

POTATOES: Slice the potatoes thinly and cut them into thin shreds about the size of matches. Deep-fry in a pan until golden. Use a slotted spoon to place the fried potato shreds in a bowl, add salt and stir. Shape towers with the potatoes and put a big dollop of butter on each piece of meat. Serve immediately while hot and smoky.

WHISKY SUGGESTION: Lagavulin 16 YO and a cold pint of lager

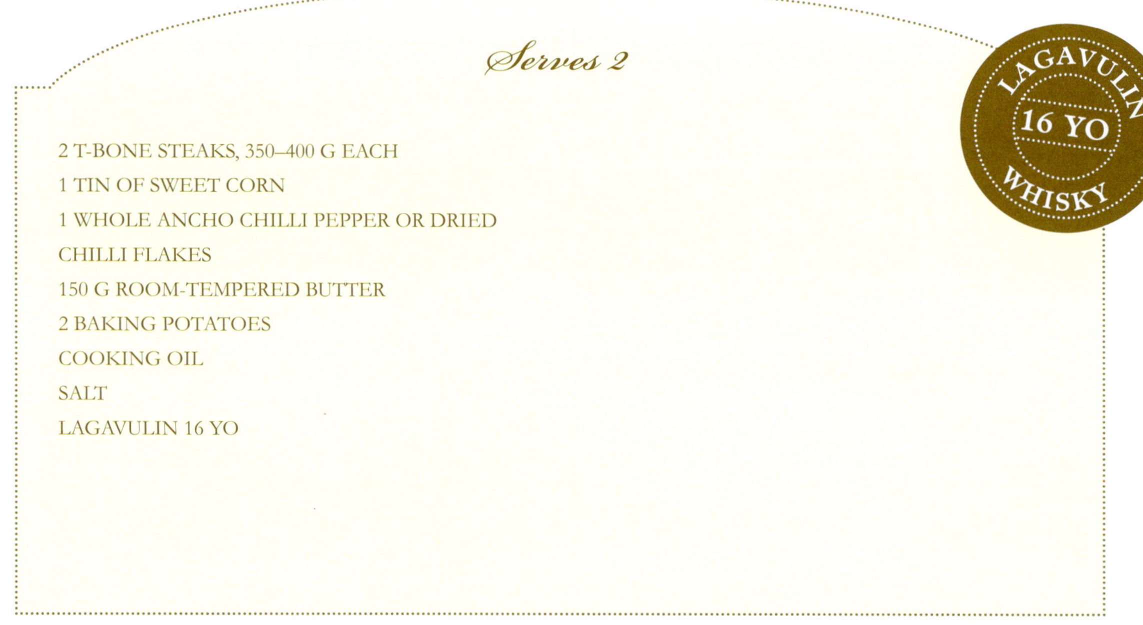

Serves 2

2 T-BONE STEAKS, 350–400 G EACH
1 TIN OF SWEET CORN
1 WHOLE ANCHO CHILLI PEPPER OR DRIED CHILLI FLAKES
150 G ROOM-TEMPERED BUTTER
2 BAKING POTATOES
COOKING OIL
SALT
LAGAVULIN 16 YO

Poached Salmon in Aromatic Stock

Instructions:

Start with the stock. Peel and chop the onion. Wash the leek and slice it thinly. Shred the celery. Combine stock, wine, whisky, onion, leek, celery, star anis, herbs and bay leaf in a pot and bring to a boil. Let simmer for approximately 8 minutes. Strain the stock and pour it back into the pot.

Sprinkle salt on the salmon and place it in the stock. Let simmer for approximately 3 minutes. Lift up the salmon and keep it warm in tin foil. Save 200 ml of the stock for serving.

Peel the carrot and cut into shreds. Slice up the courgette, maybe into tiny boats. Shred 2 of the spring onions and cut the other 2 in halves. Split the cherry tomatoes. Place the carrot, courgette and the spring onion halves in lightly salted water and let simmer for about 1 minute. Drain and mix the shredded spring onion and carrot with the dill. Reduce the stock in a small saucepan until half of the liquid remains. Add cream and butter and stir. Use a hand blender to make the sauce foamy. Place the salmon on a hot plate. Top with the vegetable shreds and pour sauce around the fish. Garnish with courgette boats, spring onion, tomatoes and serve with boiled potatoes or rice. Lovely smells from the salmon blend with aromas from the sauce and the vegetables.

WHISKY SUGGESTION: Talisker 10 YO

TALISKER 10 YO WHISKY

Serves 4

SALMON

4 SALMON FILLETS, SKINLESS AND BONELESS
½ TSP SALT

STOCK

½ YELLOW ONION
1 PIECE OF LEEK, APPROX. 100 MM
2 CELERY STICKS
750 ML FISH STOCK
150 ML WHITE WINE
2 TBSP TALISKER 10 YO
4 STAR ANISES
1 SPRIG OF THYME
1 SPRIG OF DILL
1 BAY LEAF

SAUCE

200 ML OF THE FISH STOCK
4 TBSP DOUBLE CREAM
4 TBSP BUTTER

GARNISH

1 CARROT
1 COURGETTE
4 SPRING ONIONS
6 CHERRY TOMATOES
2 TBSP CHOPPED DILL

WHISKY BEEF FILLET

Instructions:

Slice the onion and fry it in butter for about 3 minutes. Add whisky and simmer for 2 minutes.

Slice potatoes and add some stock, bay leaf and black pepper. Simmer until the potatoes are thoroughly cooked.

Thereafter, strain the liquid and add cornflour to thicken. Add the potatoes and onions again and take the saucepan off the heat.

Grill the beef fillets and after-fry until their inner temperature reaches 58°C.

Heat up the potatoes in the sauce and serve with the beef. Garnish with parsley.

This will soon become a favourite among friends and family, so make sure to make a big batch – it is a dish that inspires plentiful eating, for plenty of time!

WHISKY SUGGESTION: Caol Ila 12 YO

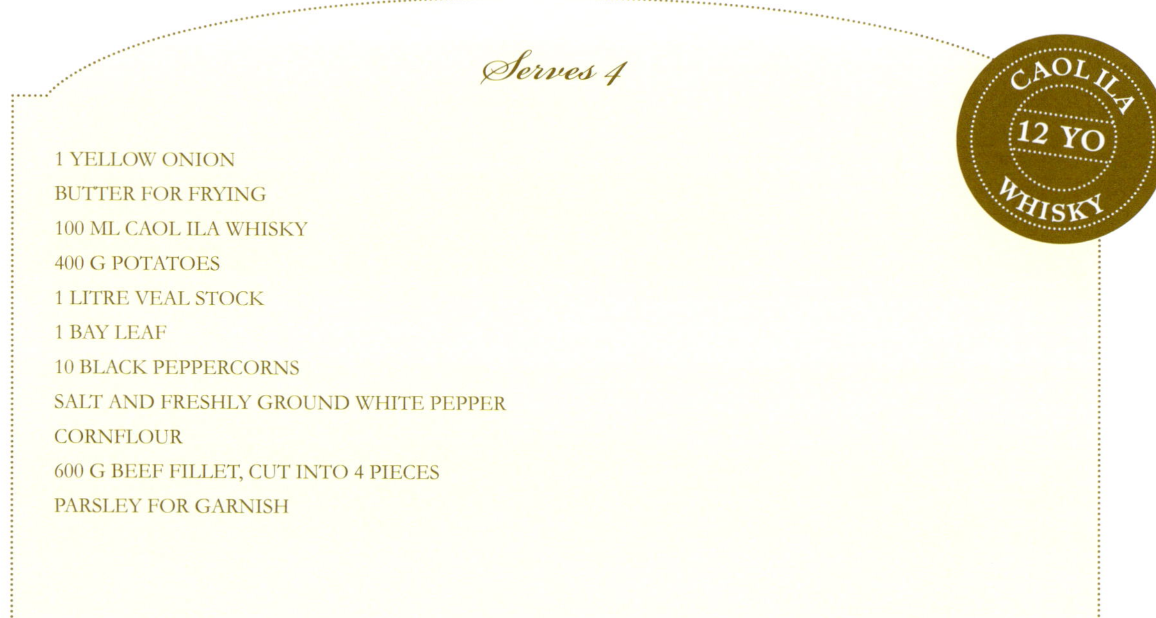

Serves 4

1 YELLOW ONION
BUTTER FOR FRYING
100 ML CAOL ILA WHISKY
400 G POTATOES
1 LITRE VEAL STOCK
1 BAY LEAF
10 BLACK PEPPERCORNS
SALT AND FRESHLY GROUND WHITE PEPPER
CORNFLOUR
600 G BEEF FILLET, CUT INTO 4 PIECES
PARSLEY FOR GARNISH

LOBSTER BRAISED IN WHISKY AND LIME SERVED WITH LOBSTER RISOTTO

Instructions:

LOBSTER: Place the lobster in boiling water for about 2 minutes in order for it to die and to make the flesh come off more easily. Split the lobster lengthwise, remove the tail and claws and remove grime if necessary.

RISOTTO: Boil the whisky until the alcohol evaporates. Add lime juice and take it off the heat.

Melt butter with garlic in a small pan and fry it until slightly brown.

Put the lobster tail and claws in the pan, add whisky and lime and cook for approximately 7 minutes. Lift up the lobster meat and let it cool off.

Bring the lobster stock to a boil. Fry the onions gently in a saucepan with a knob of butter for about 3 minutes. Add wine and cook until almost dry. Add rice and onions and stir. Add stock, a little at a time, allowing the rice to absorb the liquid gradually. Cook for approximately 20 minutes at medium heat.

When the rice is almost cooked, add the cheese to make the risotto creamy. Take the saucepan off the heat and add avocados and tomatoes.

Heat up the lobster in the flavoured butter. Spoon over lemon juice. Serve the lobster with the risotto and garnish with leaf spinach. Put the pepper mill on the table.

WHISKY SUGGESTION: Bowmore Cask Strength

Serves 4

1 LIVE LOBSTER
50 ML BOWMORE WHISKY
1 TBSP FRESHLY SQUEEZED LIME JUICE
100 G BUTTER
4 CLOVES OF GARLIC
3 SHALLOTS, CHOPPED
200 ML WHITE WINE
200 ML ARBORIO RICE (RISOTTO RICE)
1 LITRE LOBSTER STOCK
50 ML GRATED PARMESAN CHEESE
12 CHERRY TOMATOES, IN HALVES
2 AVOCADOS, IN PIECES
2 TBSP LEMON JUICE
100 ML LEAF SPINACH
FRESHLY GROUND BLACK PEPPER

WHISKY-POACHED COLD SALMON WITH POTATOES AND HERB SAUCE

Instructions:

SALMON: Lightly salt the salmon and let sit for a couple of minutes in a small waterproof dish with high sides.

Bring whisky to a boil and let simmer for 1 minute. Add water, green peppercorns, bay leaf, onion and carrot slices, and simmer for 5 minutes. Pour the liquid over the salmon and leave to cool. Put the salmon in the refrigerator and let it absorb the flavours for 3 hours minimum.

HERB SAUCE: In a bowl, whip together mayonnaise, crème fraiche, lemon juice, chives and dill. Flavour with salt and freshly ground white pepper.

Before serving, simply lift up the salmon from the liquid carefully.

Serve with half a lemon and boiled potatoes. Garnish with onion, carrot and dill. I give you my word that the neighbours will come running to find out what that lovely smell is.

WHISKY SUGGESTION: Lagavulin 12 YO Cask Strength

Serves 4

LAGAVULIN 12 YO CASK STRENGTH WHISKY

SALMON
300 G SALMON IN 4 LONG SLICES
100 ML LAGAVULIN WHISKY
300 ML WATER
10–15 GREEN PEPPERCORNS
1 BAY LEAF
1 YELLOW ONION IN SLICES
½ CARROT IN SLICES

SAUCE
50 ML LOW-FAT MAYONNAISE
50 ML LOW-FAT CRÈME FRAICHE
1 TBSP LEMON JUICE
1 TBSP CHIVES
1 TBSP DILL
SALT AND WHITE PEPPER

FOR SERVING
2 LEMONS
400 G BOILED POTATOES

DUCK BREASTS WITH GINGER AND SOY SAUCE

Instructions:

DUCK BREASTS: Start by trimming the duck breasts of all skin and sinews. Score a criss-cross pattern into the fat. Mix sugar and salt and rub it into the duck breasts. Let them rest for about an hour. Let the breasts sear in a pan; put them with the fat side facing down, no extra fat is needed. Roast in the oven at 100°C for about 15 minutes or until the meat reaches a core temperature of 56°C.

SOY JELLY: Bring the soy sauce to a boil and add the chilli sauce. Let the gelatine leaves soak for approximately 5 minutes. Squeeze out the water. Dissolve the gelatine in some of the soy mixture and stir down into the rest of the soy mixture. Pour everything into a dish covered in cling film and refrigerate until set.

SOY FOAM: Bring the ginger syrup to a boil together with soy sauce and veal stock. Add salt and pepper to taste. Take the saucepan off the heat and let it cool slightly. Add the lecithin. Blend until foamy.

NOODLES: Combine lemon juice, ginger and water in a pot. Add salt to taste. Place the noodles in the water and cook according to the instructions on the packet.

SERVING INSTRUCTIONS: Dice the soy jelly and carve the duck. Serve with soy foam, glass noodles and pickled ginger. A magnificent taste explosion with neither gunpowder nor smoke.

WHISKY SUGGESTION: Clynelish 14 YO

Serves 4

CLYNELISH 14 YO WHISKY

DUCK BREASTS
2 DUCK BREASTS
3 TBSP SUGAR
1 TBSP SALT

SOY JELLY
50 ML KIKKOMAN SOY SAUCE
2 TBSP SWEET CHILLI SAUCE
2 GELATINE LEAVES

SOY FOAM
50 ML GINGER SYRUP (USE THE GINGER SORBET ON PAGE 22, EXCLUDING THE GELATINE)
3 TBSP KIKKOMAN SOY SAUCE
2 TBSP VEAL STOCK
SALT AND BLACK PEPPER
1 TBSP LECITHIN (A NATURAL FAT BASED ON SOY, WHICH CAN BE BOUGHT IN WELL-STOCKED SHOPS)

GLASS NOODLES
1 SQUEEZED LEMON
1 TSP GRATED GINGER
500 ML WATER
SALT
½ PACK GLASS NOODLES

PICKLED GINGER CAN BE BOUGHT IN WELL-STOCKED FOOD SHOPS

PORCINI MUSHROOM SOUP

Instructions:

Start by chopping the mushrooms coarsely. Thereafter, dice the parsnip, onion and garlic finely.

Fry the mushrooms in butter for approximately 2 minutes. Add parsnip, onion and garlic and brown for a minute or two. Add cream, milk and veal stock, bring to a boil and add whisky. Add truffle oil, salt and pepper to taste.

This soup can be served with a slice of grilled lamb fillet, making it into a sturdier meal.

WHISKY SUGGESTION: Aberlour 10 YO

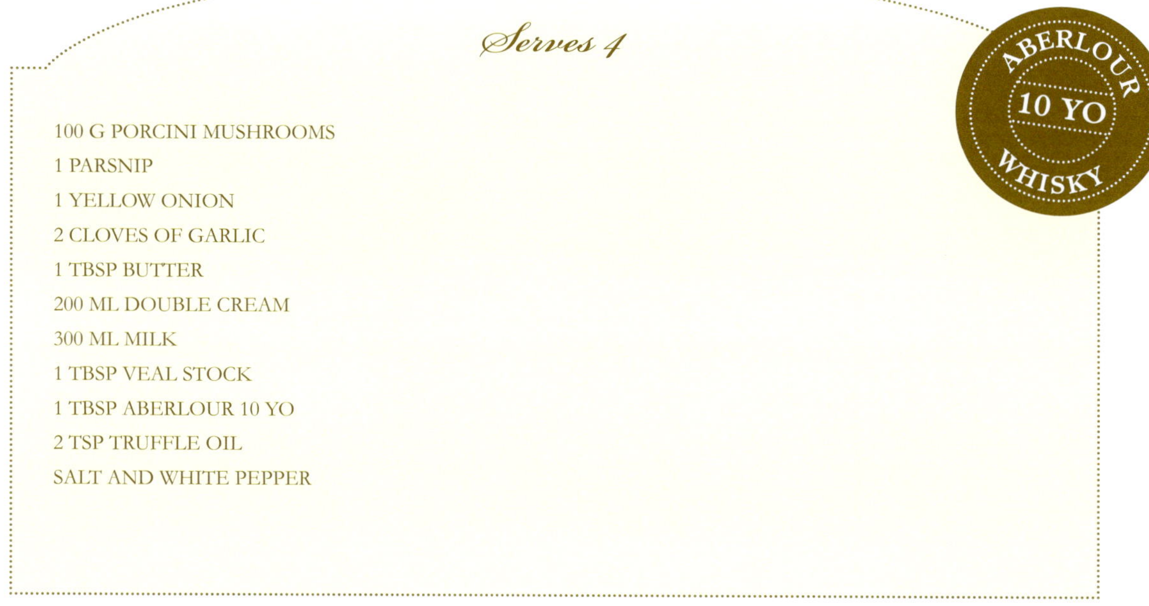

Serves 4

100 G PORCINI MUSHROOMS
1 PARSNIP
1 YELLOW ONION
2 CLOVES OF GARLIC
1 TBSP BUTTER
200 ML DOUBLE CREAM
300 ML MILK
1 TBSP VEAL STOCK
1 TBSP ABERLOUR 10 YO
2 TSP TRUFFLE OIL
SALT AND WHITE PEPPER

WILD BOAR AND MINT CROQUETTES WITH BBQ SAUCE AND COUS COUS

Instructions:

CROQUETTES: Mix all ingredients in a bowl and leave to rest for at least an hour. Form the mince into croquettes using a spoon and water. Place them in a greased oven dish and oven-fry them at 175°C for 10–12 minutes. Fry them quickly in a grill pan or in the oven grill.

BBQ SAUCE: Fry garlic and tomatoes in the butter. Add the rest of the ingredients and let it cook for at least 15 minutes. Add salt to taste.

Serve with cous cous and fresh herbs. This dish is rich and long-lasting in flavour.

WHISKY SUGGESTION: Lagavulin 16 YO

Serves 4

LAGAVULIN 16 YO WHISKY

CROQUETTES
600 G MINCED WILD BOAR MEAT
150 ML TURKISH YOGHURT
100 ML COLD WATER
1 YELLOW ONION
1 CLOVE OF GARLIC
15 G FRESH MINT
15 G FRESH GINGER
1 ½ TBSP CUMIN
SALT AND PEPPER

BBQ SAUCE
300 ML FRESH TOMATOES
1 CLOVE OF GARLIC
25 G MELTED BUTTER
50 ML TREACLE
2 TBSP BROWN SUGAR
100 ML LAGAVULIN
1 TBSP ENGLISH MUSTARD
50 ML DARK BEER
3 TBSP APPLE CIDER VINEGAR
½ TBSP WORCESTERSHIRE SAUCE
150 ML HEINZ CHILLI SAUCE
SALT

4 SERVINGS OF COUS COUS

WHISKY-BAKED LANGOUSTINES

Instructions:

Fry chopped onion and mushrooms in butter. Add cream and whisky and bring to a boil. Add chopped herbs and Dijon and give it a stir. Split the langoustines lengthwise and put them in an oven-proof dish. Top them with the mixture. Place the dish in the oven and bake on maximum heat high up in the oven for 5–10 minutes until golden. Serve with fresh lime and bread.

Fantastic aromas spread throughout the room. Set the table beautifully and watch your guests as their smiles keep broadening.

WHISKY SUGGESTION: Auchentoshan 10 YO

Serves 4

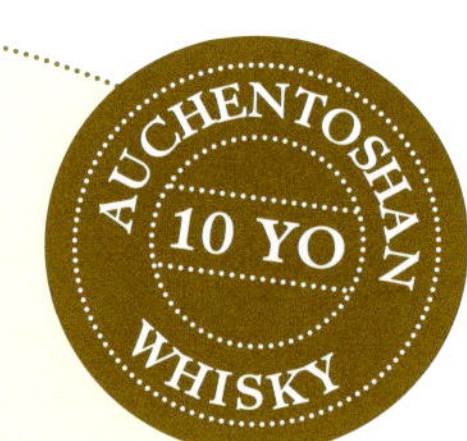

8 RAW LANGOUSTINES
6 WHITE CLOSED CUPS MUSHROOMS
1 YELLOW ONION
2 TBSP DIJON MUSTARD
50 G BUTTER
100 ML WHISKY, SWEET AND FLOWERY, AUCHENTOSHAN OR SIMILAR
150 ML DOUBLE CREAM
100 ML PARSLEY OR TARRAGON
1 EGG YOLK
SALT AND PEPPER

TRUFFLE-SCENTED ELK BOEUF SPEYSIDE WITH PASTA

Instructions:

Fry the meat in a hot frying pan in small batches and place it in a saucepan. Thereafter, fry onion, pork and carrots and add to the saucepan. Cover with wine, whisky, herbs and stock and bring to a boil. Cook everything slowly with a lid on for approximately 2–3 hours. The meat should be tender.

Lift up the meat and bring the sauce to a boil, thickening it with cornflour if necessary. Fry the mushrooms lightly and add them to the sauce. Discard the herb sprigs. Add salt and pepper and finally truffle oil according to taste.

Cook the pasta according to instructions and place it in an oven-proof dish. Distribute the meat casserole evenly on top.

Thereafter, place the puff pastry as a lid on top and add egg yolk using a kitchen brush. Place it in the middle of the oven and bake at 200°C for 10–15 minutes.

Serve immediately. Cut a small hole in the pastry lid and enjoy all the lovely aromas.

WHISKY SUGGESTION: Cragganmore 12 YO

Serves 4

CRAGGANMORE 12 YO WHISKY

800 G ELK MEAT, DICED (ELK TRICKY TO COME BY? REPLACE IT WITH BEEF)
100 G SMOKED PORK SHOULDER
1 RED ONION
2 CLOVES OF GARLIC
1 CARROT
SPRIGS OF THYME, SAGE AND BAY LEAF
SALT AND WHOLE PEPPERCORNS
300 ML RED WINE
200 ML SPEYSIDE WHISKY, E.G. CRAGGANMORE
1 BEEF STOCK CUBE
50 G BUTTER
200 ML DRIED OR FRESH BLACK CHANTERELLES
2 TBSP WHITE TRUFFLE OIL OR, PREFERABLY, FRESH WHITE TRUFFLE
2 TBSP CORNFLOUR AND COLD WATER FOR THICKENING
PUFF PASTRY SHEETS
1 EGG YOLK
200 G FRESH, THIN SPAGHETTI

BEEF CHEEK WITH TRUFFLE PUREE AND LAGAVULIN SAUCE

Instructions:

BEEF CHEEK: Peel and chop onions, garlic and carrot. Place beef cheeks in a pot together with chopped vegetables, red wine, water, nitrite salt, salt and pepper. Bring to a boil and skim off. Cook under a lid for approximately 6 hours. Lift out the beef cheek and discard the vegetables. Use the remaining broth for the sauce.

SAUCE: Bring broth to a boil. Mix water and cornflour and add this to the broth. Add whisky. Add salt and pepper to taste. If the sauce has an unpleasant colour, use sugar colouring to freshen it up.

TRUFFLE PUREE: Peel the potatoes and boil them in salted water. When cooked, add milk and butter and mix with a hand blender until smooth. Add truffle oil, salt and pepper. If desired, grate some fresh truffle on top before serving.

Serve with fresh vegetables.

WHISKY SUGGESTION: Mortlach 16 YO

Serves 4

MORTLACH 16 YO WHISKY

BEEK CHEEK
750 G BEEF CHEEK
1 YELLOW ONION
1 GARLIC
2 CARROTS
200 ML RED WINE
1 LITRE WATER
2 TBSP NITRITE SALT
2 TBSP SALT
10 BLACK PEPPERCORNS

SAUCE
500 ML BROTH FROM BEEF CHEEKS
1 TBSP CORNFLOUR
2 TBSP WATER
30 ML LAGAVULIN
SALT AND PEPPER

TRUFFLE PUREE
800 G POTATOES
200 ML MILK
50 G BUTTER
1 TSP TRUFFLE OIL
SALT AND PEPPER
(FRESH TRUFFLE FOR SERVING)

SPEYSIDE

Speyside. The name has a seductive sweet, fruity, complex and multi-faceted ring to it. There are many types of Speyside whisky, and the names of the distilleries are familiar, even world famous: Glenfiddich, Glen Grant, Glen Livet, Macallan, Cardhu, Aberlour, Longmorn, Knockando, Glenfarclas, Cragganmore, the list goes on. All of them fine and pleasant products. The glens are the beautiful setting of this geographically small area, which is, however, gigantic in the world of whisky. The local flavours have always attracted blenders, and when the major blending firms (Chivas Regal, Johnnie Walker, Ballantines and Bell's) name their favourites, Speysides are right at the top of the list. It is something about the quality of the Speyside malt that blends particularly well with other flavours. Blenders have always known it, and these days a wider audience is well aware of the fact the River Spey can contribute to appealing food and whisky combinations. I have experienced many good matches between fruity Speysides and desserts – usually incorporating chocolate in one form or another – and many recommend using Speysides for entire whisky dinners. There are subtle notes here that go with seafood as well as a robust sweetness, which is more suitable for rich casseroles and the Sunday roast. I once had the opportunity of enjoying a steaming goulash accompanied by a glass of Singleton of Glendullan. The single malt, which was served with a little chilled water in a white wine glass, was transformed into an attractive version of a full-bodied, fruity wine. Cheese goes well with Speyside malts too. I prefer mild washed-rind cheeses that are distinct but not too dominant. The nuttiness of the cheese often finds an excellent companion in a well-matured single malt that has been stored in European casks.

In the River Spey, salmon compete for size and agility. Along its banks, keen anglers are competing for the fattest and most reluctant fish. The catch and the state of the river are later discussed over a dram or two in any of the often modest watering holes nearby. In my view, salmon can certainly be enjoyed with a local label. Gravlax or smoked salmon require a full-bodied, spicy, perhaps smoky, whisky. Cooked salmon, which is often served cold with lemon and bay leaf, should be accompanied by a fruity malt with a long, dry aftertaste. In my experience, these qualities do not improve with age, so you should go for a regular bottle; why not one that has matured in an American cask?

The highland game is always honoured with a fine, well balanced dram during cooking. To sip a Macallan Fine Oak, Glenlivet Nadurra or a Cragganmore while a buck or roe deer is being slowly roasted in the oven is not bad; not bad at all in fact. Use a large wine glass and add a little cool

water. Remember that if you are serving jelly or pickles with the roast, you need to take that into account when choosing the malt. The next day you can cut off some of the drier, tasty bits and enjoy them with a Longmorn or a Glen Elgin, unless you happen to have a Benrinnes matured in European casks about!

I have deliberately chosen not to include any recipes in this chapter. You will find food that goes with Speyside single malts in all three recipe sections, as well as in the chapter about the magic of cocoa beans.

If you happen to find yourself in Speyside and in need of a drink, I can recommend the comfortable and easily accessible Highlander Inn or the Quiach Bar at the Craigellachie Hotel. I can also warmly recommend a visit to the Fiddich Side Inn. How to find it? Ask the locals – they will know.

ISLAY

I simply must include a chapter on Islay malts, of which considerable amounts are consumed in the United States and Europe, especially in Scandinavia. Bowmore and Laphroaig are global brands that can be found anywhere in the world. Lagavulin and Ardbeg are many people's number one choice, while others prefer the less smoky Bruichladdich or Bunnahabain. Caol Ila is gaining in popularity, the time of Kilchoman will come and perhaps new pagoda-head chimneys will soon appear among the rolling peat hills. Islay is a popular whisky destination, and regardless of where you are from, you will soon discover that the islanders are happy to let you call Islay your second home, although I would personally get cabin fever if I stayed too long.

The recipes and meal suggestions using Islay whisky have been composed bearing in mind the strong taste of these particular whiskies. Do not expect any subtle, blushing dew drops or frivolous, flowery spring flavours. The single malts produced on Islay are full-bodied, they bear the seal of the ocean, are often redolent of smoky peat fires and without a doubt the force of centuries. However, and this is important, hidden within each single malt are tantalising notes, which, in combination with food, may come to the fore and turn an Islay malt into a most civilised table companion.

During one of my trips, my comrades in arms created some first class meals on this island, which has become world famous for its whiskies. As I have already mentioned, you should always treat lobster and scallops with caution, but trying them is a fascinating experience since the flavours marry in subtle ways. Cheese and chocolate work very well indeed as do smoked fish and meats, not to mention oysters. My travel companions are far from the only ones to discover how to combine the mythical Islay malts with various foods and snacks.

Many of the suggestions in this book were inspired by the wide flavour spectrum of Islay malts. The basic smoky notes are developed in different ways by different distilleries. Because of this, the malt in your glass will behave in different ways even though Islay is a small island where the conditions in which the various distilleries operate are similar. What I am trying to say is that just because your bottle of Scotch was made on Islay, it does not mean that it will perform in the same way as one from the next distillery down the road. The differences are exciting and challenging to whisky aficionados.

Now a travel tip for anyone planning a visit to Islay: go to Ardbeg and have lunch there. The Kiln Café is an excellent place to stop for a bit of rest and recreation. Jackie Stewart is the enthusiastic owner. Stop off for an hour or two, enjoy lunch – with or without whisky – and take a short walk around the place. Then go down to the

ARDBEG

beach and look out over the ocean. With a bit of luck you will be able to make out the north coast of Ireland in between showers. There is no getting away from the fact that the weather on Islay does not make for a holiday in the sun. Or, as they say at Laphroaig: If you can't see Ireland you can be sure it will soon begin to rain.

I can assure you that a visit to one of the rock shelves at Lagavulin Bay in the company of a small glass of shimmering malt whisky will be an unforgettable experience. Look out over the mighty ocean, take a deep breath, allow yourself to be transported on the wings of the past and absorb the calm. Notice how the wet, briny wind seems to add to the taste of the malt. The sea somehow affects the nose and palate, turning the experience into something far from the ordinary. You can be sure that this glass of whisky will offer more than any other you have ever tasted.

If you are lucky, the sun will break through the clouds and warm up your stretch of beach, the grass and the rocks. It is an overwhelming experience. Keep your fingers crossed that a busload of tourists intent on doing the same as you are will not turn up.

As I mentioned above, a chapter on Islay was a must. Those of you who have been there need no further explanation. To those of you who are yet to go there I can only say: Tasteful journey!

Ardbeg
Old Kiln Café and Shop
Visitor Reception

Robert Burns

As I mentioned earlier, it would be a gross omission in a book that claims to manifest the connection between food, people and whisky not to include a chapter on Robert Burns and the traditional celebration of Burns's birthday on January 25, referred to as Burns Night. It is without doubt a day that is celebrated all over Scotland. Whisky clubs and other associations internationally too, have started to remember this winter's day. People get together, in more or less formal circumstances, to honour the poet who sang the praise of food and drink. Robert Burns was something of a phenomenon. He wrote and published his first poems for the apparently simple reason that he needed to finance the after-effects of a love affair. His poetry was of such a high standard that he succeeded, and he began to spend more time writing, but without forsaking romantic adventures and abundant eating and drinking. He worked for a period as an excise man – a controller of distilleries. It is not clear whether he was good at his job, but on the other hand he was a popular man in general and among Scottish nationalists in particular. His verse, steeped in the Romantic Movement, sings the praise of the good things in life. This is probably why Burns is still remembered at an annual celebration dedicated to the enjoyment of food and drink in the company of friends.

An authentic Burns Supper consists of poetry, whisky and haggis, but there are many seemingly edifying variations on this theme. My recommendation to anyone planning a Burns Night is simple and straightforward: have fun, make sure there is an alternative to the haggis, that the whisky serves its purpose and do not forget the poetry and the singing. For those who are interested, there are plenty of books and online information on the many rules and more or less important finer points of a formal Burns Night.

Burns Night Supper my way!

On arrival, the guests are allowed a few moments of gossip and catching up on the latest news, occasionally interrupted by a recital. You may choose to give each guest an assignment to perform. Offer glasses of whisky and snacks. Why not try a few of the suggestions found in this book.

When the guests are seated, it is a good idea to ask any pipers to give up their instruments, or the welcoming speech will be drowned by the noise. Keep the speech

Robert Burns

short and finish off by toasting Robert Burns in malt whisky.

Drink a large glass of water.

I suggest you start off with a soup, for example a porcini mushroom soup (page 94). Recite a poem or a song. By this time everyone will have realised that Burns Night is not something for the shy-minded.

Leave the table and take a turn around the room. Drink more water and talk about the excellent reception you experienced last time you visited Scotland.

Tap your glass to get people's attention, read the Address to a Haggis (see page 118) and then serve it – or read the Address and eat something else. Or read any poem you like from Burns's rich cornucopia and then eat something delicious. Toast in water and malt whisky throughout the meal.

Take another turn around the room. Drink more water. This time you talk about how incredibly nice it has all been so far.

Then it is time for dessert, I suggest the pannacotta on page 124. Sit back in your chair and allow the flavours to attack your palate and the warmth from you bosom to spread among your friends. Read another poem.

End the evening by fetching your best single malts. The ones you did not mean to offer your guests, but that now definitely seem to be highly suitable.

Slainté!

Brittisk torr cider
Internationell Lager
DALESIDE

HAGGIS

Instructions:

Soak the sheep's stomach in salted water, preferably over night. Turn the stomach inside out and wash it carefully. Rinse heart, liver and lungs well. Cover the liver with cold water and boil it for 1 ½ hours. After 45 minutes, add lungs and heart that have been cleaned thoroughly. Toast the oatmeal in the oven until brown and crisp.

When the offal is cooked, split the liver in half and chop one half coarsely and mince the other finely. Mince the heart and lungs. Mix everything together and add oatmeal, suet, onion, spices, lemon juice and stock. Carefully fill the stomach with the mixture, with the fatty/soft side facing inwards. Sew up the stomach, but make sure to leave enough space inside for the oatmeal to swell.

Use a needle to prick a few holes in the stomach, allowing steam to pass through and keeping it from bursting. Place the haggis in boiling water, if desired on top of the serving plate you intend to use. Boil it slowly for approximately 3 hours. It is important that the water covers the haggis throughout the cooking. When the haggis is cooked, lift it up carefully and garnish it with borecole and peppers. Cut open the haggis and distribute it to curious friends and family directly at the table.

Serve with mashed potatoes or root vegetables and vast amounts of whisky.

Serves 4–6

1 SHEEP'S LIVER
1 SHEEP'S HEART
1 PAIR OF SHEEP'S LUNGS
1 SHEEP'S STOMACH
450 G OATMEAL
450 G SUET, FINELY SHREDDED
2 YELLOW ONIONS, FINELY CHOPPED
2 TBSP SALT
1 TSP WHITE PEPPER
1 TSP NUTMEG
JUICE FROM 1 LEMON
600–900 ML RICH BEEF STOCK

ADDRESS TO A HAGGIS

by

Robert Burns

Fair fa' your honest, sonsie face,
Great chieftain o' the puddin-race!
Aboon them a' ye tak your place,
Painch, tripe, or thairm:
Weel are ye wordy o' a grace
As lang's my arm.

The groaning trencher there ye fill,
Your hurdies like a distant hill,
Your pin wad help to mend a mill
In time o' need,
While thro' your pores the dews distil
Like amber bead.

His knife see rustic Labour dight,
An' cut you up wi' ready sleight,
Trenching your gushing entrails bright,
Like ony ditch;
And then, O what a glorious sight,
Warm-reekin, rich!

Then, horn for horn,
they stretch an' strive:
Devil take the hindmost! On they drive,
Till a' their weel-swall'd kytes belyve,
Are bent lyke drums;
Then auld Guidman, maist like to rive,
"Bethankit!" 'hums.

Is there that owre his French ragout
Or olio that wad staw a sow,
Or fricassee wad mak her spew
Wi' perfect sconner,
Looks down wi' sneering, scornfu' view
On sic a dinner?

Poor devil! See him ower his trash,
As feckless as a wither'd rash,
His spindle shank, a guid whip-lash,
His nieve a nit;
Thro' bloody flood or field to dash,
O how unfit!

But mark the Rustic, haggis fed,
The trembling earth resounds his tread.
Clap in his walie nieve a blade,
He'll mak it whissle;
An' legs an' arms, an' heads will sned,
Like taps o' thrissle.

Ye Pow'rs wha mak mankind your care,
And dish them out their bill o' fare,
Auld Scotland wants nae skinking ware
That jaups in luggies;
But, if ye wish her gratefu' prayer,
Gie her a haggis!

Levin

Desserts

FEEL FREE TO KEEP THE WINE ON THE TABLE WHEN YOU BRING OUT THE CHEESE TRAY. SHERRY OR PORT MAKE EXCELLENT COMPANIONS TO DESSERTS, BUT DON'T FORGET TO SERVE YOUR GUESTS A BOTTLE OF SMOKY ISLAY MALT AS WELL – MEMORABLE TO SAY THE LEAST!

MUSCOVADO AND WHISKY FOAM WITH LIME SORBET

Instructions:

FOAM: Start by letting the gelatine leaves soak in cold water. Bring whisky, sugar and water to a boil. Remove the gelatine from the water, dissolve it in the hot liquid and leave everything to cool. Refrigerate for at least 2 hours. Thereafter, use a hand blender to mix it to a fine foam.

SERVING INSTRUCTIONS: Place one scoop of sorbet in each of four big cocktail glasses and add the foam on top of the sorbet. Garnish with cashew nuts and tagetes leaves.

Surprise friends and family by serving this refreshing creation in between starter and main course. Fun, unexpected and delicious.

WHISKY SUGGESTION: Highland Park 12 YO

Serves 4

HIGHLAND PARK 12 YO WHISKY

MUSCOVADO AND WHISKY FOAM

1 ½ GELATINE LEAVES

50 ML HIGHLAND PARK 12 YO

100 ML MUSCOVADO SUGAR

250 ML WATER

FOR SERVING

LIME, CACTUS OR LEMON SORBET

ROASTED CASHEW NUTS

TAGETES LEAVES

PANNACOTTA WITH PEACH COMPOTE

Instructions:

PANNACOTTA: Let the gelatine soak in cold water for a while. Slice up the vanilla pods and scrape out the seeds. Bring seeds, pod, cream and sugar to a boil. Stir and let simmer for 1 minute. Take it off the heat for a few minutes before adding the gelatine. Leave to cool until it starts to thicken. Discard the vanilla pod.

PEACH COMPOTE: Let the gelatine soak in cold water for a while. Rinse, split and remove the stones from the peaches. Cut into thin wedges. Put them in a saucepan with water, lime and sugar and let simmer until soft, for about 5–8 minutes. Leave to cool for a minute before adding the gelatine. Let it cool off until it starts to set.

In a glass, create layers of compote and pannacotta. After each layer, place the dessert in the freezer until set. Thereafter, refrigerate to ensure that the whole dessert is cold and completely set.

This dessert can be made a couple of days before serving. Cover the glasses in cling film to prevent the pannacotta from absorbing unwanted smells from other foods in the refrigerator.

Before serving, garnish with pomegranate seeds.

WHISKY SUGGESTION: Dalwhinne 14 YO

Serves 4

PANNACOTTA
4 GELATINE LEAVES
1 VANILLA POD
500 ML DOUBLE CREAM
50 ML CASTER SUGAR

PEACH COMPOTE
2 GELATINE LEAVES
3–4 PEACHES (APPROX. 500 G FRUIT WITHOUT STONES)
150 ML COLD WATER
JUICE FROM 1 LIME
50 ML CASTER SUGAR

FOR GARNISH
SEEDS FROM 1 POMEGRANATE

HOT CHOCOLATE AND LAVENDER CAKE WITH RHUBARB AND TALISKER CREAM

Instructions:

Start by preheating the oven to 200°C. Separate the egg yolks from the whites. Melt the chocolate in a water-bath or in the microwave. Stir down the egg yolks and the chopped lavender into the melted chocolate. Whip egg whites until fluffy with 50 ml of the sugar. Add the rest of the sugar and whip until stiff. Add a third of the egg whites to the chocolate and stir until smooth, thereafter add the rest of the egg whites.

Cover a baking tin (about 24 mm in diameter) in oven paper and grease the edges. Pour the mixture into the dish and bake in the lower part of the oven for approximately 12 minutes. Leave to cool in the dish.

Wash the rhubarb and cut it into long slices, preferably with a root vegetable peeler. Combine sugar, water and cardamom seeds in a saucepan and simmer for about 5 minutes. Add the rhubarb slices and bring to a boil. Take the saucepan off the heat and leave to cool. Whip the cream and add whisky and sugar.

Form rhubarb slices into rolls. Slice up the cake with a warm knife and distribute the whisky cream on it. Sprinkle ground cardamom on top.

A delightful dessert that requires a bit of precision, but that melts on your tongue together with the balanced flavour of whisky.

WHISKY SUGGESTION: Talisker DE

Serves 8–10

CAKE
4 EGGS
300 G DARK CHOCOLATE
1 TSP FINELY CHOPPED LAVENDER (2 SPRIGS)
50–100 ML CASTER SUGAR

RHUBARB
2 RHUBARB STALKS
2 TBSP CASTER SUGAR
150 ML WATER
6 CARDAMOM SEEDS

FOR SERVING
150 ML WHIPPING CREAM
2 TBSP CASTER SUGAR
50–100 ML TALISKER 10 YO
GROUND CARDAMOM SEEDS

COCONUT PUDDING WITH TROPICAL FRUITS IN A SWEET WHISKY SAUCE

Instructions:

COCONUT PUDDING: Bring coconut milk, cream, cardamom and sugar to a boil. Let simmer for 10 minutes, allowing the cardamom to emit flavours. Let the gelatine dissolve in the hot liquid. Strain. Pour the coconut cream into serving dishes and refrigerate until set.

WHISKY SAUCE: Bring whisky to a boil and let it simmer for 2 minutes. Add water and sugar.

Pour the sauce over all of the fruit and leave to cool. Refrigerate. Serve everything together, properly chilled.

WHISKY SUGGESTION: Caol Ila Original Cask Strength

Serves 4

COCONUT PUDDING

200 ML COCONUT MILK
200 ML DOUBLE CREAM
20 CARDAMOM SEEDS
100 ML CASTER SUGAR
3 GELATINE LEAVES, SOAKED

WHISKY SAUCE

100 ML CAOL ILA WHISKY
200 ML WATER
150 ML CASTER SUGAR
2 PASSION FRUITS, SCOOPED OUT
½ MANGO, DICED
6 LYCHEES, SPLIT AND PEELED
1 PEACH, DICED
2 PLUMS, DICED

ORANGE SORBET WITH OLIVE OIL AND SEA SALT

Instructions:

Bring orange juice to a boil and add ginger, sugar and glucose. Strain the orange syrup. Let it cool off and freeze it until it turns into sorbet, either in the freezer or in an ice-cream maker.

SERVING INSTRUCTIONS: Serve the orange sorbet with a fine olive oil and sea salt. A glorious finale to a meal – a successful combination of freshness and innovation.

WHISKY SUGGESTION: Cardhu, thoroughly chilled

Serves 4

CARDHU WHISKY

200 ML FRESHLY SQUEEZED ORANGE JUICE
1 TSP FRESH GINGER, GRATED
50 ML SUGAR
50 ML GLUCOSE

WHISKY TRUFFLE WITH WHITE CHOCOLATE

Instructions:

Cover a small dish (approximately 60 x 120 mm) with cling film. Bring cream, butter and Drambuie to a boil. Crush the chocolate and stir until melted and smooth. Pour the mixture into the dish. Refrigerate for a few hours until set. Melt the white chocolate and pipe it on top of the truffles in the dish. Cut into small squares.

WHISKY SUGGESTION: Ice-cold Clynelish 14 YO

18 mini truffles

4 ½ TBSP DOUBLE CREAM
1 TSP (5 G) BUTTER
1 ½ TSP DRAMBUIE
100 G DARK CHOCOLATE (70%)
WHITE CHOCOLATE

WHISKY AND CHEESE

There are many stories about whisky. One of them goes as follows.

In the early 1980s there was a cheese shop owner in Covent Garden who was as popular as he was full of ideas. Cheese was becoming increasingly fashionable with tourists as well as with born and bred Londoners, there was clearly a lot to choose from judging by his overflowing counter, and the customers patiently waited their turn in the crowded space. This cheese shop owner was very clever. Not only did he sell excellent produce, he also shared creative serving suggestions with his customers. People who discovered the great choice on offer also asked the owner for his serving suggestions. Towards the end of the week they would ask about what to drink with cheese, and the owner patiently dug deep into his well of experiences and delivered them as well as he could. One busy Friday afternoon he had had enough, he was a cheese salesman, for God's sake, not a sommelier! Exhausted, and maybe a little annoyed, he decided that each time a persistent customer asked for a drinks suggestion he would offer the worst he could think of. Said and done, for the rest of the day customers were informed that whisky went extremely well with cheese, so there! And not just any label would do. It had to be Laphroaig since he disliked it more than any other whisky.

On Sunday night he was lying awake in bed, imagining having to spend all Monday apologising to angry customers. Monday morning arrived, and he took a deep breath before opening the doors. All day familiar faces entered his shop, describing their experiences of the Laphroaig and cheese combination. They were all singing his praise and admiring his good taste and boldness. Smoky malt whisky and cheese was an excellent combination. If the point of the exercise was to make people stop asking for drinks suggestions, he had failed miserably. On the other hand his rash inspiration – naturally shared with other creative palates around the world – simply opened people's eyes to a pleasant flavour combination.

Is this a true story? Well, as the head of distillation at Laphroaig once told me while we were waiting to cut the spirits, 'You should know one thing, Jan; of all the lies you have heard about the whisky industry, half of them are not even true!'

HERE ARE SOME SUGGESTIONS FOR CHEESES THAT GO WITH SINGLE MALTS:

- Laphroaig with Stilton
- Glenlivet 12 YO with Dutch white goats' cheese
- Glenmorangie with Primadonna

TOMME DE CHEVRE
au lait pasteurisé
SAINT-LOUP
SURGÈRES
EN VENDEE PAR G.L.A.C.
LE MARIAGE

WHISKY AND CHOCOLATE

When you try to establish the origins of tastes and aromas, the descriptions tend to be rather technical and off-putting. Various substances are released during the different stages of the whisky-making process. These act as vehicles for aromas and molecule chains on their way to the glass, nose and palate. They may turn up as flitting revelations in your inner bank of scent memories where they evoke recollections or provoke new discoveries in a way that is unique to each individual. We are of course all conditioned to remember certain smells, and we have innate 'memories' of aromas that may have served to ease our path through childhood. During our very first year of life, we also open a unique taste and aroma account with our aroma bank, where a copy of each aroma we come across is saved. There is no great interest on investment, however, but many of these memories are vital to our very existence and for getting on in life. We are guided by our sense of smell. If we had no inner aroma bank it would be hard for us to choose the right foods, beverages and partner; and it would be tricky if the brain did not issue a warning when the smell of fire reaches our noses.

Knowing this may not make any more sense of this chapter, which is about chocolate and whisky, but learning about the diversity of chocolate from an expert may prove more interesting.

There are a number of similarities between chocolate and whisky in the way their flavours are formed. The story about the arrival of chocolate in Europe after it had awakened the curiosity of the passengers on the first ships to cross the Atlantic is one entertaining place to start. Around the same time, we find the first evidence of how the knowledge of distillation in Scotland and Ireland developed into products that may be described as drinkable, although neither was particularly popular at the time. The chocolate was raw and unrefined, and the whisky, or uisge beatha, unpredictable, to say the least. The more people that came to realise the potential of both chocolate and whisky, and as the production process improved, the more enjoyable were the end products that saw the light of day.

The fact that growing conditions affect the quality of the cocoa bean, which, in turn, affects the flavour of the chocolate, is an even more interesting revelation.

There are certain flavours and aromas in single malts that cannot be attributed to anything other than the location of the distillery, and you cannot disregard the fact that chocolate and malt whisky are both fermented products. During fermentation aromatic molecule chains are formed. Some break and others combine to form new constellations, others remain unchanged.

Consider the fact that cocoa beans taste terrible before processing. Few can

imagine that this bitter-tasting bean is capable of developing such an amazing range of flavours. The same goes for the new-make. Anyone who has sampled whisky straight after distillation cannot possibly imagine how it can be turned into anything resembling a decent beverage – ever.

Another similarity is that chocolate may be manufactured anywhere in the world where cocoa trees grow and that there are no geographical limitations to the manufacture of whisky – although most people agree that the best whiskies and, above all, the greatest diversity, is found in Scotland and South or Central America respectively. The manufacturing skills have in both cases been disseminated throughout the world, but the original regions are still at the top of the chart in terms of quality.

More interesting similarities can be found between chocolate and malt whisky. Cocoa beans may, for example, be smoked during processing. Malt, the basic ingredient of whisky, also absorbs the smoky notes from burning peat fires. And did you know that vanilla is usually added to chocolate? This can be compared to the most distinct flavours found in whisky, the ones that are added by the casks.

As everyone will have noticed, there are many delicious ways of combining malt whisky and chocolate. The wide choice of both whiskies and chocolates inspires one to go on discovering new combinations. Stacks of pralines made by different producers can be found in shops all over the world.

If I were to attempt a few suggestions, I would recommend that you do not take too much notice of cocoa content, but look for the country of origin and the name of the bean. I personally find high quality chocolate bars flavoured with, for example, sea salt, liquorice, nuts and fruits very interesting. I am fairly convinced, too, that most fine chocolate sellers are real experts and that they run excellent establishments. This means that if you take your time when shopping for chocolate, there is a good chance you will succeed. I guarantee that there are countless amazing, rich combinations waiting to be discovered. Regardless of what you choose, I know from experience that the chocolate/malt whisky combination is unequalled and outstanding.

PURO

Young, slightly sweet and flowery whiskies such as Balblair 1997 should be sampled in combination with 60% fruity, slightly sweet chocolates. Try the vintage brands Gran Couva or Palmira from Valrhona.

Rich and flowery whiskies with salty notes such as Springbank 10 YO or Talisker 10 YO are some of my favourites in combination with dark, pistachio and salt flavoured chocolate creams. The pistachio/salt/dark chocolate combination is heavenly in combination with the whisky.

A full-bodied, smoky, sweet whisky such as Lagavulin 16 YO is the most difficult to combine. You might try a 70% French Pralus made from Java beans or some other brand from the same area. It is very smoky indeed, almost like bacon. Or try a bitter tart coffee cream to match this robust single malt.

Medium rounded, slightly smoky and sweet whiskies such as Oban 14 or Ardmore Traditional Cask are highly recommended for dark, slightly bitter and slightly sharp 70% chocolate, for example Ocumare from Chocovic.

News from Grenadine Publishing

THE COCKTAIL BOOK

By Eliq Maranik

Fancy a cocktail party? Mix all your favourite cocktails at home! We bring you our own big book of cocktails, distilled out of our best recipes, useful tips and cocktail knowledge. With more than 250 different cocktail recipes, there is something for everyone – the novice as well as the more experienced home bartender. You will find the old familiar cocktails in many new guises, often with an international, exciting flavour. The cocktails vary in number of ingredients and complexity of preparation, but they have one thing in common – they're delicious!

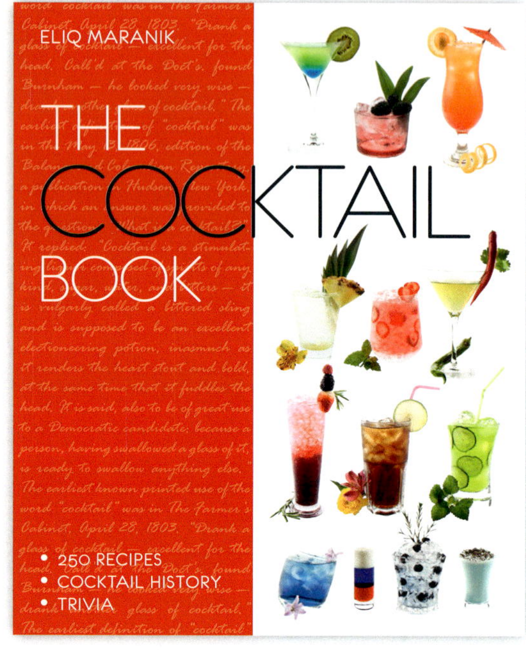

ISBN: 978-1-908233-05-9
PUBLICATION: 30 September 2011

In addition, *The Cocktail Book* includes a section on glass types and equipment and advices you on which spirits, liqueurs and juices to use. You will also find a thorough guide to all the technical terms and expressions used in bartending, a comprehensive history of alcoholic beverages and a fascinating account of the manufacturing of spirits.

Each drink recipe is accompanied by trivia and fun facts, often relating to the historical people and myths surrounding the drinks. There simply can be no cocktail book without Mr Hemingway!

In short, this a complete collection of cocktails ideal for surprising your friends on a Saturday night, but also for boosting your own cocktail skills and knowledge!